Grant's Last Battle

THE STORY BEHIND *THE PERSONAL MEMOIRS OF ULYSSES S. GRANT*

by Chris Mackowski

Chris Mackowski, series editor
Kristopher D. White, chief historian

The Emerging Civil War Series

offers compelling, easy-to-read overviews of some of the Civil War's most important battles and stories.

Recipient of the Army Historical Foundation's Lieutenant General Richard G. Trefry Award for contributions to the literature on the history of the U.S. Army

Other titles in the Emerging Civil War Series by Chris Mackowski:

Don't Give an Inch: The Second Day at Gettysburg, July 2, 1863—from Little Round Top to Cemetery Ridge
by Chris Mackowski, Kristopher D. White, and Daniel T. Davis

Fight Like the Devil: The First Day at Gettysburg, July 1, 1863
by Chris Mackowski, Kristopher D. White, and Daniel T. Davis

Hell Itself: The Battle of the Wilderness, May 5-7, 1864
by Chris Mackowski

The Last Days of Stonewall Jackson: The Mortal Wounding of the Confederacy's Greatest Icon
by Chris Mackowski and Kristopher D. White

A Season of Slaughter: The Battle of Spotsylvania Court House, May 8-21, 1864
by Chris Mackowski and Kristopher D. White

Simply Murder: The Battle of Fredericksburg, December 13, 1862
by Chris Mackowski and Kristopher D. White

Strike Them a Blow: Battle Along the North Anna River, May 21-May 26, 1884
by Chris Mackowski

That Furious Struggle: Chancellorsville and the High Tide of the Confederacy, May 1-4, 1863
by Chris Mackowski and Kristopher D. White

For a complete list of titles in the Emerging Civil War Series,
visit www.emergingcivilwar.com.

Also by Chris Mackowski:

Chancellorsville's Forgotten Front: The Battles of Second Fredericksburg and Salem Church, May 3, 1863 by Chris Mackowski and Kristopher D. White

Seizing Destiny: The Army of the Potomac's Valley Forge and the Civil War Winter that Saved the Union by Albert Z. Conner, Jr., and Chris Mackowski

Grant's Last Battle

THE STORY BEHIND *THE PERSONAL MEMOIRS OF ULYSSES S. GRANT*

by Chris Mackowski

SB

Savas Beatie
California

Second edition, first printing

ISBN-13: 978-1-61121-160-3

Library of Congress Control Number: 2015943486

SB

Published by
Savas Beatie LLC
989 Governor Drive, Suite 102
El Dorado Hills, California 95762
Phone: 916-941-6896
Email: sales@savasbeatie.com
Web: www.savasbeatie.com

Savas Beatie titles are available at special discounts for bulk purchases in the United States by corporations, institutions, and other organizations. For more details, please contact Special Sales, P.O. Box 4527, El Dorado Hills, CA 95762, or you may e-mail us as at sales@savasbeatie.com, or visit our website at www.savasbeatie.com for additional information.

For Terry Rensel,
my Evil Twin

Author's Note

As kids, my brother and I had a poster of the presidents on the closet door in our bedroom. My brother picked Lincoln as his favorite. I picked Ulysses S. Grant. I liked how grand the name sounded, and I knew he smoked cigars, which also seemed grand. That was about the extent of my knowledge, though.

My first *real* introduction to Grant came as it did for Robert E. Lee: in the Wilderness of central Virginia. There, I learned about the "dust-covered man" who had vowed that there would be no turning back. I have since spent a great deal of time on that battlefield, as well as the ones at Spotsylvania and North Anna, sharing stories of Grant's time in the east. I have also visited the sites of his major battles out west. I have come to admire him a great deal.

I often liken Grant to another of my favorite characters from the war, Confederate General Stonewall Jackson. Both were men of deep resolve. I have seen how their resolve played out dramatically—and in dramatically different ways—on the battlefields around Fredericksburg, Virginia. Grant's final 15 months likewise demonstrate his resolve, and in an especially striking way. That's what has always drawn me to the story.

At the Jackson Shrine, where Stonewall Jackson died, a clock sits on the fireplace mantel in Jackson's death room (left), just as one sits on the fireplace mantel in Grant's death room (right). The Jackson clock still ticks on, while the Grant clock was stopped at the time of death and never restarted. Occasionally, a visitor will come into the Shrine and see the clock and ask, "Have you ever seen the one at Grant Cottage?" (cm)(gc)

I've also been drawn to that story as a writer, particularly one who has studied and practiced memoir. Memoir is a particularly tricky form of nonfiction, not reliant on facts but on larger truth. "Truth derives from facts but is not dependent on them," says historian Joan Waugh. "It is based in the facts but ultimately not answerable to them. Today, professional historians call truth 'Interpretation.'"

Grant was especially meticulous about his fact-checking, but what he writes and what he doesn't, and what conclusions he draws from those facts, are all products of memoir, not of history writing. "By deciding to give his work the full title, *Personal Memoirs of Ulysses S. Grant*," says historian Charles Bracelen Flood, "he did himself a great favor. He could write about the things he wished to put before the reader, and omit those things he did not. At one stroke, he relieved himself of the obligation to include everything he might know about a battle or a person, while reserving the right to dwell on a smaller matter or fleeting perception."

Grant's doors stand twelve feet tall and now serve as the main entryway into Stevenson Ridge's largest events space, the Lodge. (cm)

I own a first edition of the *Memoirs*, but I have another connection to Grant's story, as well. When Grant was general in chief of the army during Andrew Johnson's administration, he and Julia lived in a Washington, D.C., townhouse at 205 I Street NW near the capitol (Sherman lived in #203). Julia Grant referred to it as "this lovely house, this magnificent home." Eventually, however, the entire row of townhouses was demolished to make way for Interstate 395. The wooden doors from the Grants' townhouse found their way, years later, to Stevenson Ridge in Spotsylvania, Virginia—my wife's family's property. Every day, I walk through the same doors Grant himself passed through.

The story of Grant's last battle has been told by others, and I strongly encourage you to read their accounts. My take, in introducing you to these events, will be slightly more personal, keeping in the spirit of both history *and* memoir. By sharing it in such a way, I hope to help you connect with Grant's story in the kind of personal way I have connected with it, too.

Notes About the Text

Material in quotation marks, including dialogue, represents direct quotations from primary sources. Dialogue that appears in italics rather than quotation marks is based on indirect quotes from primary sources.

Grant's former aide, Horace Porter, said Grant "spelled with heroic audacity, and 'chanced it' on the correctness." I have left Grant's spelling intact, which at times looks like typos (and which has sometimes left me sleepless, such as when I left "too" as "to," as Grant wrote it). I feel compelled to point out Grant's heroic audacity with spelling in order to preserve the honor of my capable proofreaders and copyeditors.

Table of Contents

Footnotes for this volume are available at
http://emergingcivilwar.com/publications/the-emerging-civil-war-series/footnotes

PHOTO CREDITS: Architect of the Capitol (aoc); Rita Bergendi (rb); civilwaralbum.com (cwa); New York State, Office of Parks, Recreation, and Historic Preservation—Grant's Cottage State Historical Site (gc); Adam Badeau's *Grant In Peace* (gip); *Frank Leslie's Illustrated* Newspaper (fl); *Harper's Weekly* (hw); Historical Marker Database (hmdb); John Lopez (jl); Library of Congress (loc); *Lincoln, Grant, Sherman, Farragut: An Account of the Gift, the Erection and the Dedication of the Bronze Statues Given by Charles H. Hackley to the City of Muskegon, Michigan* (lgsf); Chris Mackowski (cm); Jennifer Mackowski (jm); pereiradasilva.home.sapo.pt (pds); John Groo for The Mark Twain House & Museum (jg/mthm); National Park Service (nps); New York Public Library (nypl); Bob Perring (bp); Frank Scaturro (fs); Bruce Schulze (bs); Pat Tintle (pt); U. S. Grant Boyhood Home (usgbh); Waymarking.com (way); Wikipedia (w)

The tree-lined plaza at Grant's Tomb offers a welcoming approach. (cm)

Acknowledgments

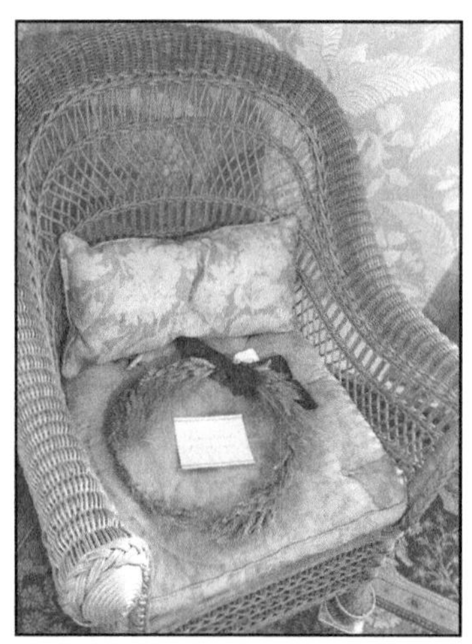

Grant's favorite chair now sits in the corner of his death room at Grant Cottage. (cm)

My greatest debt for this book-about-a-book goes to my uncle, James Cawley, the man who taught me what a wonderful thing it is to love books. He had a marvelous personal library; when I was a kid, it had a sacred air about it. On a trip to the beach when I was in early middle school, he bought me a copy of Frank Herbert's *Dune* at a used book store (apparently the beach didn't offer sand enough), and that did it for me. I have loved books, and loved reading them, ever since.

My aunt, Mary Beth Perring, has been the other great reader in my life. She and I have always shared a similar sensibility in books, which was great nourishment to me for years. I thank her and her husband, Bob—my Uncle Buck—for the photography they contributed to this book.

While writing a book about writing a book, I have thought often of the people who taught *me* how to write books. In particular, I thank Gail Cummings, Holly Dworken Cooley, the late Welch Everman, Kurtis Scaletta, Mark Van Tilburg, Kenny Fries, Paul Selig, Jane Wohl, the late Lisa Barnett, Leslie Heywood, Maria Maziotti Gillan, and Patrick Vecchio.

At Grant Cottage, I am grateful for the patient attention from former executive directors Mary Faith Martini and Jonathan Duda; Site Interpreter Samantha Dow; the President of the Friends of Grant Cottage, Tim Welch; and most especially volunteer (and internet curator) William Underhill and living historian/tour guide Steve Trimm. I am grateful, too, to the many volunteers who shared their expertise, stories, and exuberance. Grant's memory is in wonderful hands.

Frank Scaturro and Ed Hochman with the Grant Memorial Association also made contributions to this project. Ed's hospitality in New York is always a pleasure. Thanks, too, to the National Park Service at Grant's Tomb (officially the Ulysses S. Grant Memorial). In an adrenalized city like New York, they ensure that the tomb still offers a distinctive respite.

I appreciate the historians kind enough to contribute appendices to this volume: Edward Alexander, Jim McWilliams, Kathleen Logothetis Thompson, Patrick Tintle, and my own former college history professor, presidential scholar Dr. Richard Frederick. Frank Varney, who contributed the foreword and whose work I greatly admire, wrote a must-read book on Grant's memoirs that gets at the heart of history vs. memoir: *General Grant and the Rewriting of History: How the Destruction of General William S. Rosecrans Influenced Our Understanding of the Civil War.* ECW's Chief historian, Daniel T. Davis, continues to provide research assistance and advice, and my partner in crime, Kristopher D. White, continues to serve as an invaluable sounding board; I am deeply indebted to both of them.

At St. Bonaventure University, I thank my dean, Dr. Pauline Hoffmann, and the departmental assistants, Kathy Boser and Suzzane Ciesla. I thank our team of work-study students, who do a lot of photocopying for me, and I thank my own students for their patience and support. I hope Grant's story is a reminder to them that writing *should* be hard work but that it does, indeed, matter.

Lastly, I thank my family, especially my children, Stephanie and Jackson, and my wife, Jennifer.

Although I traditionally save my final thanks for my family, I do have one last note. In the course of writing the first edition of this book, one of my wife's friends and colleagues, Gail Brimer, was diagnosed with throat cancer. Not a day went by that her struggle didn't remind me of what Grant and his family must have been going through. His was not some distant, abstract story; it was immediate, human, and real. I am grateful to Gail for keeping me in touch with that. Her story is still being written, but I'm glad to report that all indications now suggest a much happier ending.

Sculptor John Lopez makes Grant an accessible figure on the streets of Rapid City, South Dakota, as part of the city's "City of the Presidents" public sculpture project, all funded through private donors. A limited number of castings of the statue are available, as well (www.johnlopezstudio.com). (JI)

For the Emerging Civil War Series

Theodore P. Savas, *publisher*
Chris Mackowski, *series editor*
Kristopher D. White, *chief historian*
Sarah Keeney, *editorial consultant*

Maps by Hal Jespersen
Design and layout by Chris Mackowski

Foreword

BY FRANK P. VARNEY

Before the dust had even settled, before the smoke of battle had even cleared away, participants in the greatest of American conflicts began trying to shape how the Civil War would be remembered. They met with varying degrees of success, but it is probably safe to say that no one had as much influence on how the history of the war would be remembered as did Ulysses S. Grant.

Those of you who have read my book dealing with Grant's *Memoirs* know that I am not certain that this was a positive thing. Grant was not at all shy about castigating his personal enemies, about praising his friends, or even about inventing things that buttressed his particular—and sometimes peculiar—version of history. But we need to consider just why Grant was so successful at shaping history when so many others were not. Why, we must ask, have his memoirs never gone out of print, never stopped influencing historians, when the writing of so many others has receded into the mists of time?

For one thing, Grant's writing was clear, concise, and to the point: the very model of what historical writing should be, in some ways – if you are willing to overlook his tendency to massage the facts at times. He possessed a grace and clarity of style that make his writing very approachable. There is also the sense of looking over the shoulder of a great man as he struggles to win his battle against mortality just long enough to get his words down on

The front porch of Grant Cottage on Mt. McGregor in Wilton, New York, offers a contemplative window into Grant's last days. (cm)

paper. For Grant's last battle was against an enemy that none of us can defeat.

As I have publicly stated in other venues, Grant's memoirs have become one of the most frequently-quoted sources for many Civil War historians: too frequently, in fact. If you pull off your library shelf a book on Grant's generalship, or a study of his campaigns, or even a biography of Grant, you may find that most of the footnotes refer to Grant himself. It is certainly appropriate, when studying Grant, to refer to his own writings. What is less appropriate is when historians rely on Grant's own analysis in order to draw conclusions.

Ulysses S. Grant deeply valued personal loyalty, and he was fiercely loyal to those who showed loyalty to him—sometimes to a fault (as in his presidency). Understanding Grant's attitudes about loyalty serves as an important lens for anyone who reads his memoirs. (loc)

Fortunately, that trend may be changing. I was one of the early voices questioning this trend, but mine is not the only one. Chris Mackowski, David Powell, David Moore, Robert Girardi, Paula Walker, Diane Monroe Smith, and others are also examining Grant's campaigns with an eye to what other participants have said about them—and, like me, they are finding that there is much more to the story.

But that still does not bring us to the answer: how important is Grant's *Memoirs*, and how has it stood the test of time? The answer to the first is "very." Although depending on Grant as the final word on anything can be risky, he still was one of the most important figures of the Civil War. Failing to consider his words when studying that period would be a significant oversight. It is important to remember, however, that there is much more to the story than Grant's version. We know that for any other memoir, yet for some reason some historians seem to forget that basic, fundamental caution when they deal with Grant. But even so, he was at the center of some of the greatest events of history, and his eyewitness account is certainly valuable.

To the second question there are several possible answers. First, as mentioned previously, the *Memoirs* are very well written. They possess a narrative flow that draws the reader in, and they are remarkably easy to understand. Grant never succumbed to the urge to write in jargon that would be inaccessible to all but professional soldiers. Second, they provide a unique insight into the workings of a great mind under unimaginable stress. There is a seductive danger in assuming that what Grant tells us about others is true; but there is no doubt that Grant is telling us a great deal about himself, in ways he may not have even realized.

Finally, the incredible drama of the act of writing is impossible to ignore. I have visited the Grant Cottage several times and have also spoken there. The lovely setting masks the tragedy that played out there. Grant was a dying man in great pain, racing the clock in order to bequeath to his family something other than the legacy of debt that his wretched lack of business acumen threatened them with. Many of us, faced with the pain and drugged torpor he dealt with, would simply have given up: Grant, as he so often did, persevered and overcame. And in the process he bequeathed to all of us a precious gift: the thoughts of a great, if imperfect, man.

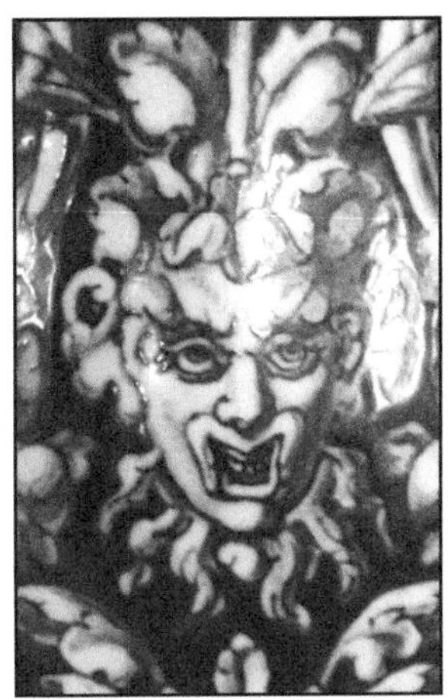

The clock in Grant's death room has two faces: the more traditional face that tells the time and this one, which may be mirthful or may be sinister. (cm)

FRANK VARNEY, PH.D., ***is the author of*** **General Grant and the Rewriting of History: How the Destruction of General William S. Rosecrans Influenced Our Understanding of the Civil War.** ***A graduate of William Paterson University and Cornell University, he is an associate professor of U.S. and Classical History at Dickinson State University.***

"If I succeed in telling my story
so that others can see as I do
what I attempt to show, I will be satisfied.
The reader must also be satisfied,
for he knows from the beginning
what to expect."

— Ulysses S. Grant

"I will have to be careful about my writing.
I see every person I give a piece of paper to
puts it in his pocket. Some day they will
be coming up against my English."

— Ulysses S. Grant

Prologue

May 24, 1864

"There will be no turning back," said Ulysses S. Grant shortly after he crossed the Rapidan River in early May 1864. As commanding general of all Union armies, Grant had chosen to tag along with the Army of the Potomac, which had just found itself embroiled in battle with Robert E. Lee's Army of Northern Virginia in the vast, "dark close wood" of central Virginia's Wilderness.

Previous Union commanders who had taken their lumps at Lee's hands had withdrawn to lick their wounds and resupply, reinforce, and reequip. Grant refused. "I intend to fight it out along this line if it takes all summer," he told Washington.

And so he did, using march and maneuver to get around Lee when he could not hammer his way through: from the Wilderness to Spotsylvania Court House, to the banks of the North Anna River then Totopotomoy Creek, to Cold Harbor, across the James River to the gates of Petersburg, and inexorably—by hammering "continuously against the armed force of the enemy and his resources, until by mere attrition, if in no other way, there should be nothing left to him"—to Appomattox Court House.

While Grant did smoke cigars—and more often just chewed on them—a newspaper report following the fall of Fort Donelson in early 1862 mentioned that Grant liked cigars. They began pouring in as gifts. Grant gave away most of them, but he began smoking more of them, too. By the spring of 1864, he was up to as many as 20 cigars a day. (cm)

"[I]n battle, after giving an order, he never doubted, or wished to recall it," an aide later said. There was no second-guessing, no contradicting, no going back.

After the surrender of the Confederacy's

Ulysses S. Grant (left) was born on April 27, 1822 in Point Pleasant, Ohio. His wife, Julia Dent (right), was born on January 26, 1826, just outside of St. Louis on a small plantation called White Haven. The couple met through Julia's brother, Frederick, who was a West Point classmate of Grant's. Julia and Ulysses married on August 22, 1848, after a four-year engagement, and they remained deeply devoted to each other for the rest of their lives. They eventually had four children: Frederick Dent Grant, Ulysses S. Grant, Jr. ("Buck"), Ellen Wrenshall Grant Sartoris ("Nellie"), and Jesse Root Grant. The Dent family homestead—where the couple met and later lived—is now preserved as the Ulysses S. Grant National Historic Site. The portraits above are on display there. (rp)

principal army, the road led Grant to Washington, D.C., and two terms as president of the United States. "It was my fortune, or misfortune, to be called to the office of Chief Executive without any previous political training," he said in his farewell address to Congress. "It is not probable that public affairs will ever again receive attention from me further than as a citizen of the Republic. . . ."

Afterward, he and his wife, Julia, took a two-and-a half year 'round-the-world tour. A reporter who went on the voyage was startled by the almost instant transformation that overcame Grant. "That reticence which had characterized the manner of the Ex-President during the many years of his onerous and toilsome employment in the service of his country, dropped from him as though it were a mask. . . ."

Partway through the journey, Grant—who had never been adroit with finances—discovered he had miscalculated the cost of the trip and suddenly found himself strapped for cash. But again, there was no turning back. Rather than return to America, he wired to his son who sent financial reinforcement.

Grant and Julia adjusted their accommodations and continued on in more modest style.

They had the time of their lives. Leaders and dignitaries from around the world feted him as an unofficial ambassador of the United States, the great hero of the age on a goodwill tour. "I cannot help feeling that it is my country that is honored through me," he told one adoring crowd.

"Grant the World Traveler" (loc)

Years later, he admitted to an old friend that the trip helped him better appreciate the work of America's founders and the importance of the preservation of the Union. "I know, as I did not before, the value of our inheritance."

Even in 1880, when the possibility of a third term as president tempted Grant to return to the political arena, there was no going back. At the Republican National convention, his overconfident political operatives botched his nomination, which went instead to the compromise candidate James Garfield. "Individually, I am much relieved at the result, having grown weary of constant abuse," Grant later told one of those operatives.

The 1880 Republican National Convention (loc)

As early as 1883, publishers had asked Grant to write about his military experiences, but he always turned them down. A former assistant, Brig. Gen. Adam Badeau, had already published *The Military History of Ulysses S. Grant* with Grant's blessing. "I have always intended that General Badeau be the last word," Grant continually insisted. "I have nothing else to add." Even when it came to revisiting his own past, it seemed, there was no turning back.

He had fixed his eyes forward ever since he was

Grant, chomping on a cigar, ordered the Army of the Potomac forward from the Wilderness in May of 1864. "I intend to fight it out along this line if it takes all summer," he announced. There would be no turning back. (loc)

young. "One of my superstitions had always been when I started to go any where, or do anything, not to turn back, or stop until the thing intended was accomplished," Grant once admitted.

> *I have frequently started to go places where I had never been and to which I did not know the way, depending on making inquiries on the road, and if I got past the place without knowing it, instead of turning back, I would go on until a road was found turning in the right direction, take that, and come in by the other side.*

There was no turning back.

But everything changed for Grant on June 2, 1884—and it all changed because of a peach.

Facing financial difficulties, Grant and his immediate family had retired to their summer cottage in Long Branch, New Jersey, a fashionable neighborhood on the Jersey shore. That early summer day was warm, but Grant found the cool ocean breeze pleasantly refreshing. He had just come in and saw, on the table, a bowl of fruit.

"There was a plate of delicious peaches on the table, of which the General was very fond," Julia recalled. "Helping himself, he proceeded to eat the dainty morsel; then he started up as if in great pain and exclaimed: 'Oh my, I think something has stung me from that peach.' He walked up and down the room and out to the piazza, and rinsed his throat again and again. He was in great pain and said water hurt like fire."

In fact, in the ordeal ahead, drinking water would continue to be one of his most painful experiences. "[N]othing gives me so much pain as swallowing water," he later admitted. "If you can imagine what molten lead would be going down your throat, that is what I feel when swallowing."

It was cancer—throat cancer—and it was severe. A doctor consulted on the case looked at Grant's test results and declared, "General Grant is doomed."

And so the great war hero was about to begin the battle of his life: the battle *for* his life. Once more he would draw on his battlefield experience, but in a wholly new way—one that would give proof to the old adage that the pen was, indeed, mightier than the sword.

3
AUTO SPRINKLER SHUT
OFF LOCATED

The Fall

CHAPTER ONE

MAY 4, 1884

Ferdinand Ward was a sociopath, but no one knew it at the time. The charismatic 30-year-old would spend the whole rest of his life swindling, bullying, and scheming people out of their money. He would be, says historian—and descendant—Geoffrey C. Ward, "perpetually unrepentant, uninterested in anyone's troubles but his own."

But on the morning of Sunday, May 4, as he knocked on the front door of 3 East Sixty-Sixth Street in midtown Manhattan, everyone still thought of Ward as "The Young Napoleon of Wall Street." Tall, thin, unconquerably charming, he had enjoyed a meteoric rise in Manhattan's financial circles and, in the process, had made many men rich—very rich. Everything he touched seemed to turn to gold. He regularly offered investors returns as high as 40 percent, and his investment firm held the highest possible ranking.

The former location of the Grants' townhouse at 3 East Sixty-Sixth Street in Manhattan (left) is marked today by a plaque on the wall (above). (jm)(jm)

On this morning, he had come to the townhouse of one of his business partners, former president of the United States and savior of the country, Gen. Ulysses S. Grant. Grant, who had given up his military pension to take the presidency and who had, subsequently, retired from the office with virtually no money, now enjoyed a plush lifestyle thanks to Ward's financial genius. Grant's initial $100,000 buy-in into their joint venture, the investment firm Grant & Ward, had ballooned to $750,000. The former general's newfound wealth and his enduring prestige allowed him to move among the highest circles of the country's rich and powerful.

Grant himself did little more at the firm than sign whatever papers Ward put in front of him, pay attention to his other business, and entertain visitors. "By the contract of co-partnership Mr. Ward alone had the right to sign the firm name and he alone had the key [and] combination to the vault," Grant later explained to a friend. Grant had contributed his considerable reputation to the firm but left the finances to his young partner. "I am willing that Mr. Ward should derive what profit he can for the firm that the use of my name and influence may bring," Grant once said.

Ward explained the potential embarrassment that faced Grant & Ward while Ulysses (sitting) and Buck (standing) listened. As usual, Grant took the news stoically with a mind toward fixing the problem as he understood it. The Grants had no idea that Ward himself was the real problem. (gip)

"Mr. Ward insisted that the business management should be left solely to him," said another of the firm's partners, Grant's son, Ulysses S., Jr.—"Buck." "I had the greatest confidence in him and I consider him to be a very able man." He was, after all, the Young Napoleon of Wall Street, credible and incredible at the same time. No one disputed his authority, Buck said; no one questioned his judgment.

Daily, Ward lined up 20 cigars on Grant's desk—a smoking tradition the general had started 20 years earlier during the Civil War—and otherwise left Grant to his own devices. "[He] sat in his familiar chair and smoked his cigar," one visitor later recounted. "He was so hearty and genial in his manner that no one could fail to like him and feel drawn to him."

But today, Ward needed Grant's help. Ushered into the first-floor parlor, Ward broke Grant's Sunday morning calm.

The firm was in trouble.

New York City's treasury had withdrawn a considerable amount of money from Marine Bank, owned by another of Grant & Ward's partners, James D. Fish. "We have six hundred and sixty thousand dollars on deposit there," Ward explained. "It would embarrass us very much if the bank should close its doors."

To ensure the bank opened on Monday morning, and thus avoid embarrassing the firm, Ward had, thankfully, rallied some $250,000 to help cover the bank's shortfalls. Could Grant somehow secure the other $150,000? Fish, embattled as he was by the treasury's withdrawal, could not. The firm's fourth partner, Grant's son, dabbled in the office's day-to-day operations, but mostly, he attended to his own law practice. In any event, he didn't have the ability to leverage so much money in such a short time under such troubling conditions.

Ferdinand Ward's baby face belied a brilliant mind—although it wasn't brilliant in the "financial wizard" kind of way people believed. Rather, he was a brilliant con. (gc)

Only Grant could do it.

Grant was famously impassive in the face of troubling news of any sort. As Ward outlined the firm's financial pinch, Grant listened stoically, then assented to help. Grant left his young partner in the parlor as he sallied forth. He'd see what he could do.

On that same day 20 years earlier—May 4, 1864—Grant set forth from his field headquarters near Culpepper Court House, Virginia, to begin the campaign that would ultimately define his career. Now, he had no way to know that he was once more setting forth on another campaign—one that would ultimately define his legacy.

Ulysses S. "Buck" Grant married Fannie Josephine Chaffee in 1880. Fannie was the daughter of Senator Jerome Chaffee of Colorado, and Buck's marriage to her helped cement the Grant family's reputation in social circles. (loc)

* * *

In an era of extravagant beards, William Henry Vanderbilt had one for the ages. His mutton chops extended outward like two brillo wings that formed perfect triangles. Like nearly everything about him, they made him seem larger than life. Being one of the wealthiest men in America helped, too.

Vanderbilt would have had little opportunity to befriend a tanner's son from Galena, Illinois—even one who'd become president of the United States—were it not for Grant's financial success since settling in New York in 1881. That, coupled with Grant's reputation as the general who'd saved the country, had earned Vanderbilt's respect and,

The palatial Vanderbilt mansion stretched from 51st to 52nd streets in Manhattan. (loc)

William Henry Vanderbilt, who was about to celebrate his birthday on May 8, was reportedly the world's richest man. (loc)

over the ensuing months, Vanderbilt's friendship. "He is one of us," Vanderbilt once declared.

In the wake of Ward's troubling news, Grant sought out Vanderbilt for assistance. He calmly and clearly laid out the problem.

"I care nothing about the Marine Bank," Vanderbilt replied. "To tell the truth, I care very little about Grant and Ward. But to accommodate you personally, I will draw my check for the amount you ask. I consider it a personal loan to you, and not to any other party."

Later, after the fall, Grant would refuse money from friends and strangers alike—his pride too staunch to accept charity. But here, now—Grant saw this as just a matter of business. He would be able to repay the loan in a day or two—a week at most. When Wall Street heard that Vanderbilt himself had floated the money to support Marine Bank, it would quiet all nerves, such was the strength of Vanderbilt's reputation and pocketbook.

Grant thanked him politely and headed back home, where his partner awaited.

* * *

I often wonder about Ward, sitting there in the Grant parlor as Grant sought out friends willing to help. Accounts don't say how long Grant was gone, although he made at least one other stop before Vanderbilt's. Nor do accounts say what Ward did during the time Grant was gone—only that Grant left him there when he set out and found him there on his return.

But Ward is slippery, as rogues are wont to be, difficult to pin down. One account has him riding in the carriage alongside Grant, coaching him where to go. Another has Grant giving him Vanderbilt's check first thing Monday morning rather than Sunday afternoon on his return. Another has Buck delivering the check.

The Grant parlor resembled a fine arts museum, with vases, furniture, ornaments, and other knick-knacks they had assembled during their around-the-world voyage. (nypl)

Ward was the kind of man whose wheels never stopped churning. Once, while poking through the house, he found a vase full of $20 gold pieces—$800 worth. He talked Mrs. Grant into investing the money in Grant and Ward rather than let it sit in the vase and not earn interest.

The home was "laden with curios and rich gifts—the spoils of the Grants' tour around the world," Ward once said, describing an almost museum quality to the place. Gild-frame paintings hung on the walls, with cabinets and shelves to hold brick-a-brack. There were so many vases, some sat on formal parlor chairs, while others sat on the fireplace mantel. An ornate oriental rug filled the center of the floor.

When the Grants purchased the home, Ward brokered the deal. "It was a much larger and more expensive house than we had intended (or had the means) to buy," Julia later wrote, "but it was so new and large that this quite outweighed our more prudential scruples—unfortunately, as later I had to pay out of the proceeds of General Grant's book a mortgage of fifty-nine thousand dollars on it."

Ward had taken the Grants' house payment and, instead of buying the brownstone outright, spent only enough to leverage the mortgage. He misappropriated the rest—just as now, sitting in the

"We are comparative strangers in New York City; that is, we made it our home late in life," Grant one day observed to Julia. They didn't move to the city until 1880 and didn't move into their brownstone on East Sixty-Sixth Street until the autumn of 1881. "It was a much larger and a more expensive house than we had intended (or had the means) to buy, but it was so new and sweet and large that this quite outweighed our more prudential scruples," Julia later recounted. Despite their late-in-life arrival, the Grants received a warm welcome from New York, which the former president never forgot. When he eventually decided on a place to be buried, he chose New York because "the people of that city befriended me in my need."(gc)

parlor, he plotted to make off with whatever money Grant came back with.

How confident was he that Grant would succeed? What plan—if any—did he have for that money? Was he already cooking up his next scheme? Planning his next swindle? It's perhaps too much to think of him twirling the tips of his moustache and, inside, laughing sinisterly, but his descendant, Geoffrey Ward, has planted the seed: "Ferdinand Ward appeared only as a stock villain," the historian observed of Ward's role, "insinuating himself onstage just long enough to ruin the ex-president and his family, then disappearing. . . ."

But on some level—even if sparked only by self-concern—the frenetic strain of the shell game had worn Ward down. He felt frazzled. He'd lost weight. The air was being sucked right out of him.

* * *

On Monday, May 5, Grant pulled up to the firm's office at 2 Wall Street to no sign of trouble. He went upstairs and went about his business.

Downstairs, Buck smelled a fish. Ward had come to him to explain that the money his father had rounded up the previous day wasn't enough, after all. "Now, take it coolly, old boy," Ward said, "don't get excited, and remember that we don't want our names to go down, and we will fight before it comes."

Buck chose not to tell his father but, instead, gathered the company's portfolio and sought advice. First on the list: Jay Gould, another of the country's wealthiest tycoons, who looked over the investments and declared them worthless. Next: Buck's attorney, Stanley Elkins.

We need to pay a visit to Mr. Ward, Elkins suggested. *We need to find out from him why Mr. Gould thinks the firm's investments are worthless.*

Buck and Elkins arrived at Ward's around seven p.m. He's not at home, Mrs. Ward said.

We'll wait, Elkins replied—and the two men sat in Ward's parlor much as Ward had sat in Grant's the day before.

Five hours passed. Finally, Ward appeared in his slippers. The firm is fine, he assured them.

If that was so, said Elkins, then certainly Ward wouldn't object to writing a check to another of Elkins' clients, Buck's father-in-law, Sen. Jerome Chaffee. Four hundred thousand dollars would cover Sen. Chaffee's initial investment, he believed.

Certainly, Ward said. The check will be available in the morning.

Outside, Elkins expressed his suspicion. "Did you observe Ward had his slippers on?" he asked. "He was in the house all the time and was afraid to come down and see us."

Grant's physical condition was already compromised when his financial condition collapsed. On Christmas 1883, Grant had suffered a fall from his carriage, seriously injuring his hip. By May, he still hobbled on crutches. "[T]he unusual confinement somewhat affected his spirits, though not his intellect," an aide said. "He was the most patient of sufferers, the most equable of prisoners." (gip)

* * *

The bouncing began the next morning, as soon as Marine Bank opened. It refused Ward's check and closed its doors—forever, as it would turn out. Other banks refused to cash checks drawn on Ward's accounts, too.

By noon, an angry crowd had congregated outside 2 Wall Street. When Grant pulled up in his carriage, he saw Buck, beleaguered, trying to fend them off.

"Marine bank closed this morning," Buck tried to explain. "Ward had fled. We cannot find our securities. Father, everything is bursted, and we cannot get a cent out of the concern."

Twenty years earlier, during the battle of the Wilderness, Grant sat beneath a tree and whittled as he waited for news of the fight. The pile of shavings at his feet grew, and he stripped away the fingertips of his gloves. Similarly, after the first day of the battle of Shiloh in April of 1862, he weathered a rainstorm beneath the boughs of a tree while waiting for the chance to let the battle play itself out. On May 6, 1884, he sought refuge in his upstairs office and waited for events to unfold. Like couriers on the battlefield, Buck, and the firm's cashier, George Spencer, brought him updates throughout the day.

"Spencer," Grant finally asked, "how is it that man has deceived us all in this way?"

JE 17676144 A
E5
THIS NOTE IS LEGAL TENDER
FOR ALL DEBTS, PUBLIC AND PRIVATE
Treasurer of the United States
SERIES
2009
GRANT

CHAPTER TWO

MAY 1884

"I think the condition of the country on the whole is quite satisfactory," Grant told the St. Louis *Post-Dispatch* on the morning of May 6. The paper, in turn, told readers Grant had made his pronouncement "before the news of the financial difficulties in Wall Street had reached him." Perhaps Grant had jinxed himself in saying so.

Save for 80 dollars in his pocket and another 130 Julia literally pulled from a cookie jar that evening, Ward's financial chicanery had left Grant destitute. "Imagine the shock to us, who thought we were independently wealthy!" Julia exclaimed.

The collapse rippled through the Grant family well beyond the walls of 3 East Sixty-Sixth Street. "[L]ike a thunderclap," Julia later said. "It was a great shock to my family, as they all believed they were not only prosperous but wealthy." All of the Grants' children had invested various amounts in the firm, as had Buck's father-in-law, Senator Chafee. Combined, the family was out nearly a million dollars.

"Yes, I am absolutely penniless," Grant's eldest son, Fred, told reporters. "Ward has ruined us all."

As Buck later explained the totality of the ruin, "None of us liked to keep a dollar out of the firm that was not absolutely needed, because we thought that we were losing when we kept money that might be earning a very heavy profit. So confident were we all that Grant & Ward were making piles of money that we invested everything we could get."

It is ironic, perhaps, that Grant—who had such financial trouble—found himself on the $50 bill. He first appeared on $50 notes in 1913. (cm)

Grant thought the firm was $2,800,000 in the

black, with another $1,300,000 of securities in the vault. He believed "Ward to be worth 1,000,000 of Dollars himself alone."

But Ward had been shuffling money out the door as soon as it came in. In effect, he was running an elaborate Ponzi scheme, using investments from one person as dividends to pay off another. Ward greased the wheels by covertly telling investors that Grant was using his influence to affect government contracts; in fact, Grant never did any such thing and had expressly forbade Ward from ever making such suggestions.

In the days following the collapse of Marine Bank and Grant & Ward, Wall Street panicked and investors—some worried, others outraged—flooded the streets. (loc)

In the end, the scale of Ward's fraud was staggering: nearly $16.8 million by the time the red ink stopped bleeding.

"I am looking for something to do. . ." a glum Fred told reporters. "That will depend upon whether or not anything is saved from the wreck."

* * *

The day after the collapse, Grant returned to 2 Wall Street. "The General looked weary and troubled, and declined to see anybody except the most intimate friends," the *New York Times* reported. The unfolding crisis shook him badly. During those drawn-out hours, Grant would "suffer for hours in his large armchair, clutching nervously with his hands at the arm-rests, driving his fingernails into the hard wood," a confident later revealed.

Outside the smoke-filled office, Grant tried to keep a brave front. To his sister, Jennie, he wrote on May 8 about "the great disaster to the firm of Grant & Ward." "We are all well, and are trying to be happy," he assured her. "Do not be the slightest uneasy."

Easier said than done. "I could bear all the pecuniary loss if that was all," Grant wrote privately to his friend George Childs, "but that I could be so long deceived by a man who I had such opportunity to know is humiliating."

That man, Ward, was holed up in his own office at 2 Wall Street. Buck, who confronted him there on the same day the *Times* described Grant as "troubled," found Ward in "a state of intense nervous excitement, weeping and wringing his hands in distress." Humbled and penitent, Ward admitted his perfidy—"a wicked thief and a great rascal, robbing, cheating, and deceiving him and the other members of his family from first to last."

Buck snapped, *The least you can do is tell the truth about the matter.*

I will, Ward promised.

Later, when trying to explain himself to investigators, Ward—looking "deathly pale"—said he "simply borrowed from Peter to pay Paul . . . [borrowing] money at a high rate of interest to pay debts previously contracted." He admitted the other partners knew comparatively little about it.

Co-conspirator James Fish began squabbling with Ward almost as soon as the bottom fell out. "[S]ome days after the bank had closed its doors, Ward came to the bank while I was there," Fish told a reporter, "and we had an interview in one of the upper rooms. . . . It was a hot one, I can tell you. I said things to him that I would not like any man to be able to truthfully say to me." (gc)

So it was that the newspaper headlines began to evolve after news of the disaster broke. They went from "Drawing checks . . . with no funds to meet them" to "Is Grant Guilty?" to, finally, suggestions of woeful ineptness. Opposition papers hinted that naivety equated to criminal neglect.

"You can rest assured . . ." Fred declared, "that while father has a cent in the world it will be employed in cancelling his indebtedness."

The first debt Grant turned his attention to was the $150,000 check Vanderbilt had written him over the weekend. Vanderbilt insisted on forgiving it, but Grant refused, offering his brownstone as payment instead—but then everyone discovered Ward's mishandling of the mortgage. The Grants didn't actually own their home. "He was penniless in the house that was crowded with his trophies," a confident later said.

The Grants quickly began selling other properties: in Washington, Philadelphia, Chicago, and Galena. "[A]nd last, though not least, the dear old homestead in Missouri, White Haven," Julia recalled. "When I signed this last deed, it well-nigh broke my heart. My tears fell thick and fast; I could not help it."

The entire family soon planned a strategic withdrawal to their summer home at Long Branch, a resort town along the Jersey shore some 30 miles to the south. Fred, who had also lost his house in the collapse, moved in with the Grants with his wife and two children—"a very happy arrangement for all," Julia confessed.

* * *

In the end, it was Grant's army that saved him. First in ones and twos, then by the thousands, the former soldiers of the United States Army sent their former commander notes, well wishes, and huzzahs enough to make their throats sore.

In the midst of the flood of letters came a check—$500—came from a man Grant had never met, Charles Wood of Lansingburgh, New York. "[M]y share due for services ending about April 1865," Wood wrote.

Mexican Ambassador Mathias Romero, a close friend since Grant's presidency, visited East Sixty-Sixth Street shortly after hearing news of the financial collapse. On his way out, he surreptitiously left $1,000 on a table in the Grants' foyer, knowing that if he gave it to the Grants directly his friend would refuse it. (w)

"The money at this time would be of exceeding use to me," Grant answered, "having not enough to pay one month's servant hire, or room if I were to leave my house, and nothing coming in until the First of August."

Wood's response was to send another $1,000. Consider it a loan, he said to spare Grant's pride, to be repaid at your convenience.

"You have conferred an obligation more than I can ever repay," a gracious Grant responded. "The money of course I do not doubt but I can return. . . . You in the generosity of your heart have relieved [my] anxiety."

Andrew J. White, an American living in London, also offered $1,000. "Your course in these personal matters shows the same self sacrificing spirit you evinced during the war for the good of the country," he said.

Marion Lake, the postmaster in Fayette, Missouri, predicted, "if need be every true soldier will Donate." He urged Grant

> *not to let this little misfortune cast one shaddow over you. . . . I am poor but stand ready to divide with you. . . . do not hesitate if any thing is wanting, we are ready to comply. . . . we stand firm, and Ready & willing to do our part.*

The demonstrations of support continued to grow. On May 13, the town of Ithaca, New York, started a subscription drive on Grant's behalf. "It is intended that everyone in Ithica shall subscribe $1 and no more," the announcement said. "A snug little sum is expected to be reached by this means for the hero of Appomattox. . . ."

Then came a stunning show from the veterans on May 31. The city of Brooklyn celebrated Decoration Day, and Grant, along with General in Chief of the Army, Grant's one-time protégé Phil Sheridan, was saluted as the guest of honor. "A salvo of cheers that for a time almost rendered inaudible the booming of the cannon burst from thousands who thronged the street . . ." the *New York Times* reported. "[T]he cheering was simply deafening."

On June 11, Brooklyn welcomed him back for the annual meeting of the Society of the Army of the Potomac, a veterans group that selected Grant as its next president. "I accept the trust you put in me today, and feel highly flattered that you have selected me, one who has never been more than an honorary member of your society, to preside over you," Grant told them. "But after all, twenty years ago, our relations were intimate and close."

The veterans leapt to their feet, threw their hats in the air, and gave not just three cheers but nine.

On July 31, Grant accepted an invitation from his friend, the New York philanthropist George Stuart, to visit a reunion of the United State Christian Commission, meeting over the first three days of August in Ocean Grove, New Jersey, just a few short miles from Grant's cottage at Long Branch. The charitable organization had done much during the war to provide for the soldiers and tend to the wounded. "I had special opportunities to know of service rendered, of consolations administered by the side of deathbeds; of patient, unswerving attention to the sick; of letters written to the mourning parents of noble sons . . ." said Grant, who then broke down during his speech. The enthusiastic reception from the war's "better angels" moved him too deeply to finish.

By late May, Ward (lampooned on the cover of *Puck*, on the right side of the illustration) was in the Ludlow Street Jail. "My time is mostly employed in working on my papers," he wrote. "I am well treated by my keepers, and I try to keep up my spirits as best I can under the circumstances." (loc)

"And so it was everywhere," Julia later said after one of her husband's appearances. "How the men shouted at his entrance! How they stamped and shouted and cheered when he arose to say a few words to them!"

It did not matter what the newspapers said about him after all, Grant realized. His men had not lost faith. And in showing their admiration and enthusiasm, they sustained him.

HEADQUARTERS
GENERAL U. S. GRANT,
NIGHT OF APRIL 6, 1862.
GENERAL GRANT IN HIS MEMOIRS SAYS:-
"DURING THE NIGHT RAIN FELL IN TORRENTS AND
OUR TROOPS WERE EXPOSED WITHOUT SHELTER.
I MADE MY HEADQUARTERS UNDER A TREE A FEW
HUNDRED YARDS BACK FROM THE RIVER BANK."
THE LARGE OAK TREE REFERRED TO, STANDING
WHERE THIS MARKER NOW STANDS, WAS DE-
STROYED BY CYCLONE OCTOBER 14, 1909.

CHAPTER THREE

EARLY JUNE 1884

Robert Underwood Johnson had a great idea.

The 31-year-old editor of *Century Magazine* wanted to publish first-person accounts from some of the most prominent men to fight in the American Civil War. His project, which he saw as an "important historical enterprise," would eventually evolve into *Battles & Leaders of the Civil War*—one of the standard go-to resources for any military historians of the Civil War. Published in 1887, *Battles and Leaders* ranks with the Official Records of the War of the Rebellion, the Southern Historical Society Papers, and a handful of memoirs as foundational texts for research.

Johnson required Grant-like doggedness to get his idea to come to fruition, however—and the largest obstacle seemed to be Grant himself.

Grant was the obvious choice to lead off the *Century*'s series. Lincoln had been assassinated before the war even ended, and Lee had died in 1870. That left Grant as the most prominent surviving man of the conflict. As such, the *Century* reached out to Grant in January of 1884 with an invitation to contribute.

He turned them down flat.

"His declination was so decisive it left us without hope," Johnson later admitted. The magazine later requested an interview but "made no progress in this flank attack upon the General's position," either, Johnson said.

At the battle of Shiloh in April of 1862, Confederates caught Grant's Army of the Tennessee by surprise and, after a day of intense fighting, nearly drove them into the Tennessee River at Pittsburg Landing. Approached that evening by a shaken William T. Sherman, Grant responded, "Lick 'em tomorrow." Reinforced overnight, Grant did indeed lick the Confederates the next day, turning disaster into victory. (cm)

Robert Underwood Johnson and Ulysses Grant shared an interest in conservation. Grant, as president, established Yellowstone National Park in 1872—the first national park in the world. Johnson would use his power with *Century Magazine* and, later, with *Scribner's Monthly*, to champion similar efforts. For instance, he played a key role with naturalist John Muir in establishing Yosemite National Park as well as the Sierra Club. (gc)

"He seemed indifferent to his past career, and certainly was glad to be out of controversies of war and politics," the young editor observed. "He did not possess that historic sense of a man-of-letters which impels one to make up the record of an active life."

Indeed, had the collapse not come on Wall Street, Grant might never have considered revisiting his past at all. Years earlier, he had approved the work of one of his former aides, Brig. Gen. Adam Badeau, who had published the three-volume *Military History of Ulysses S. Grant* in 1881. "It is all in Badeau," Grant told Johnson.

But the collapse *did* come, and Grant found himself penniless. Johnson and his colleagues at the *Century* saw a possible opening. Rather than make a headlong approach, though, they appealed to Badeau's literary vanity and asked him to serve as an intermediary.

"The country looks with so much regret and sympathy upon General Grant's misfortune that it would gladly welcome the announcement and especially the publication of material related to him or by him concerning a part of his honored career in which everyone takes pride," the *Century* wrote. The country would be glad, the note continued, to have its attention diverted from Grant's troubles by such an account, "and no doubt such diversions of his own mind would be welcome to him."

I'd be glad to have you send a representative to discuss the matter, Grant replied, much to Johnson's "surprise and joy." Johnson traveled to Long Branch, New Jersey, to conduct most of the negotiations in person.

Like Grant, Johnson had migrated to the Jersey shore to begin the summer, albeit for less fiscally sand-like reasons. From Point Pleasant, the early June journey to Long Branch was easy and the day beautiful. Long Branch, Johnson said, "had the charm and emptiness of a summer resort whose season had hardly begun." The Grant cottage, when he arrived, also felt empty. "[T]here was a lonely air about the simply furnished cottage," he said.

Grant, who "frankly and simply" admitted to Johnson his dire financial condition, said "his changed financial condition had compelled him to reconsider what resources might be afforded by his pen."

Built in 1866, the cottage at Long Branch became a favorite destination for Grant's family during his presidency—so much so that it became known as the summer White House. Julia appreciated the cottage's "health-giving breezes and its wide and restful piazzas." (loc)

Johnson offered Grant $500 per article, hoping initially for four pieces: Shiloh, Vicksburg, the Wilderness, and Appomattox (which would eventually be swapped out for a piece on Chattanooga instead). Grant said the financial arrangement sounded perfectly acceptable.

Johnson left feeling both elated and deflated. "[H]e gave me the impression of a wounded lion . . ." the editor later recounted of his visit. "I left him with a deep impression of his dignified sorrow, his courage, and his greatness."

* * *

Johnson wasn't the only person angling for Grant's pen. In November of 1883, publisher Alfred D. Worthington of Hartford, Connecticut, had approached Grant about writing a memoir about his war experiences or his round-the-world voyage, predicting royalties of at least $25,000 within two years. Grant demurred. "I feel much complimented by your proposition but I schrinck from such a task," Grant said.

Just weeks after the collapse of Grant & Ward, Worthington made another overture. "I would have no objection to seeing you at any time that might be convenient to you, and talk upon the subject you write about," Grant replied. "But I do not feel equal to the task of collecting all the data necessarily to write a book upon the War, or of my travels." Worthington, apparently content to let the matter drop, never visited.

The Grants with their youngest son, Jesse, enjoy a summer afternoon at Long Branch in 1872. (loc)

As it soon turned out, Grant didn't seem equal even to the task of writing his magazine articles. The first draft of his first piece—an account of the April 1862 battle of Shiloh—arrived in the *Century* office on July 1. It read almost exactly like—and as dryly as—Grant's original official report of the battle.

Johnson immediately recognized it as "this new disaster of Shiloh."

"The General . . . did not realize the requirements of a popular publication on the war," Johnson wrote, recalling the editorial team's "dismay." "This required all the tact that I could muster, that he should not be discouraged, and at the same time our project should be saved. . . ."

Johnson tucked the draft in his coat pocket and made the trek back out to Long Branch.

Again, Johnson took a sideways tack. Rather than talk about the article, he drew Grant into a conversation about the battle. "General Grant, instead of being a 'silent man,' was positively loquacious," Johnson recalled. Grant talked for hours.

This is exactly what the article should try to capture, Johnson told him. People had already been able to read the official report. What they wanted were Grant's thoughts, perspectives, and personal experiences—"the personal touch that makes a great battle a vital and interesting human event." Think of it like a talk one would make to friends after dinner, Johnson said.

Grant seemed astonished at this, but grasped the difference immediately. Once more he set to work.

Two weeks later, Grant sent a revised draft of the article to Johnson's office. Like the second day at Shiloh, the second draft of Shiloh went much more in Grant's direction.

* * *

Grant's critics over the past century and a half love to dismiss him for being a one-trick pony on the battlefield. *He only knew how to make headlong attacks*, they sneer. *Even when they were futile, he just kept attacking headlong.*

In fact, one of the things I have grown to admire about Grant most was his ability to learn from mistakes on the battlefield and his willingness to try new things based on the lessons he learned. He was notoriously stubborn, but that played out as a dogged refusal to quit, not as head-against-the-wall futility. The seven unsuccessful attempts he made at Vicksburg before his final—successful—campaign illustrate his determination well. His chess match with Lee during the 1864 Overland Campaign illustrates it, too.

Johnson discovered the same was as true for Grant the writer as it had been with Grant the general. "[N]o one ever had an apter pupil," the young editor later wrote.

Or a more eager one, apparently, too. Even as he'd begun revising his Shiloh article, Grant "commenced on the Vicksburg campaign." In a letter to Adam Badeau, Grant said he'd "made considerable progress so far as pages covered. But I have not gone far from my base."

That Grant was pleased by his work is evident in the tone of his letters to Badeau over the next few weeks—talking about his progress, engaging in wordplay based on military references, and offering his "kindest regards." But Grant had also learned from the hard lesson of his first Shiloh draft. He wanted Badeau's practiced eye—as a professional writer and as the *de facto* keeper of Grant's literary military legacy—to look over the *Century* articles.

"I do not think I will be able to get through the *Wilderness* before you go to the Mountains," Grant punned, referring to a trip Badeau was about to make before coming to Long Branch. "But I will take Vicksburg, and I will be glad to see you here. In fact, I do not want to submit my Article until you have approved it."

It's easy to see Grant feeling out of his depth, leaning on a trusted friend and adviser for support in this wholly new endeavor. But as events would unfold, Grant would get his feet under him in a wholly unexpected way—and he would quickly outgrow the need for anyone's approval but own.

"THE GENERAL DID NOT REALIZE THE REQUIREMENTS OF A POPULAR PUBLICATION ON THE WAR."

The Writer

CHAPTER FOUR

SUMMER 1884

Shiloh. Vicksburg. The Wilderness. Chattanooga.

"All that summer was spent by my dear husband in hard work: writing, writing, writing for bread," wrote Julia.

And the more he wrote, the more he liked it. Although "a man not inclined to sedentary occupations," Grant worked as many as seven hours a day writing. "He at once became interested in the work," Badeau later recalled. "The occupation distracted him from the contemplation of his misfortunes, and the thoughts of his old companions and campaigns brought back pleasanter recollections."

But that wasn't all, Johnson noted. "He got out of the writing not only diversion from his troubles but the happiness of finding that he could do something new," the editor observed. "He said to me once: 'Why, I am positively enjoying the work. I am keeping at it every day and night, and Sundays.'"

Living not far down the coastline made it easy for Johnson "to follow the course of his progress in the untried field of authorship," something he later considered "one of the fortunate experiences of my life, since it revealed to me the heroism and the integrity of a much misrepresented man."

Once Grant started writing, he found he had a knack for it. "Happy, happy thought for him!" Julia realized. (cm)

But that's the great secret of Grant's writing: it was not an "untried field" at all. Grant's military service had honed his writing to crisp clarity. "There is one striking feature about Grant's orders," an army staff officer once wrote: "no matter how hurriedly he may write them on the field, no one ever has the slightest doubt as to their meaning, or ever has to read them over a second time to understand them."

Grant, seated in the center, surrounded by his inner circle from the war: Eli Parker, Adam Badeau, Orville Babcock, and Horace Porter. Parker would go on to serve in the Grant administration as the commissioner of Indian affairs. Badeau would serve in a variety of official posts and launch a successful literary career. Babcock would serve as the chief of staff in the Grant White House and found himself at the center of numerous controversies and charges of corruption. Porter would serve as President Grant's personal secretary and, in 1897, would write his own wartime memoir, *Campaigning with Grant.* (nps)

That clarity of thought and articulation reflected a writing style that was "vigorous and terse, with little of ornament," wrote Grant's one-time aide, Horace Porter. "[I]ts most conspicuous characteristic was perspicuity. . . . No document which ever came from his hands was in the least degree pretentious. . . . Whatever came from his pen was grammatically correct, well punctuated, and seldom showed an error in spelling."

At least in official documents, that is. In personal correspondence, Porter admitted Grant "spelled with heroic audacity, and 'chanced it' on the correctness."

Grant would eventually come to this important realization about his writing on his own: "I have to say that for the last twenty-four years I have been very much employed in writing," he would one day write to Badeau.

> *As a soldier I wrote my own orders, plans of battle, instructions and reports. They were not edited, not was assistance rendered. As president, I wrote every official document, I believe, usual for presidents to write, bearing my name. All these have been published and widely circulated. The public has become accustomed to my style of writing. They know that it is not even an attempt to imitate either a literary or classical style; that it is just what it is and nothing else. If I succeed in telling my story so that others can see as I do what I attempt to show, I will be satisfied. The reader must also be satisfied, for he knows from the beginning what to expect.*

As a writer, I see particular irony in that last line: like so many other writers, Grant began his *Century* articles *thinking* he knew what to expect, but somewhere along the way, the project began to take on a life of its own. What began as an effort "undertaken simply to keep the wolf from the door" began to morph into something more.

* * *

By early August, Grant finally understood that he had more on his mind than just the four articles. "I intend . . . now that I have commensed to it, to go on and finish all my connection with the war of the rebellion whether I publish it or not," he wrote to a friend. "If it pleases me when completed I probably will publish it."

Johnson had told Grant that the *Century* would take as many articles as he'd be willing to produce, so he certainly had a venue for anything he wanted to say. But the magazine, despite how the editors had been treating him, just wasn't a big enough platform. "I do not think I care to write any more articles, for publication, than I have already agreed to write for the Century," Grant wrote Johnson. "These will form as much of the complete series,—which I intend to write, whether published or not—as ought to go into print at this time."

As soon as Grant's first article appeared, *The Century*'s circulation jumped dramatically. (loc)

Grant's first article, "The Battle of Shiloh," eventually appeared in the February 1885 issue, immediately boosting the *Century*'s circulation just as the editors had intended. "Vicksburg" appeared in the September 1885 issue, "Chattanooga" in the November 1885 issue, and "Preparing for the Wilderness Campaign" in February 1886. In acknowledgement of the articles' success, the

Philadelphia newspaperman George Childs had no financial stake in Grant's writing whatsoever and so served Grant well in the role of adviser because he had plenty of publishing experience. Childs proved to be one of Grant's most stalwart friends. (loc)

Century would increase the fee it paid Grant, then increase it again: $4,000 per article.

By the time the articles began appearing, though, Grant would be on to another, grander project. His correspondence with Johnson offered a clue: "at this time"—the operative phrase. Giving the *Century* notice would free him from any further obligation to them and allow him to think broader.

As it happened, the *Century*'s publisher was thinking along those very same lines.

* * *

"Do you really think anyone would be interested in a book by me?" Grant asked.

He was lunching with Johnson and Johnson's boss, Roswell Smith, president of the *Century*, who had come to Long Branch to talk "book." Joining them was Grant's friend and Long Branch neighbor, Philadelphia newspaper publisher George Childs. The four sat on the cottage veranda, enjoying the early afternoon breeze off the ocean. The day was charming.

"General," Smith replied, "do you not think the public would read with avidity Napoleon's personal accounts of his battles?"

The answer, as Grant well knew, was *Of course*.

Johnson described Grant's initial question as naive, "for he was entirely free from affectation," yet Grant's question strikes me as at least somewhat disingenuous. He knew, by the time he sat down to break bread with Johnson and Smith, that he was on to something. He had also heard a summer's worth of wild cheers from the veterans, who had heartily sustained him even after the collapse of Grant & Ward. They, if no one else, would be interested; they, if no one else, would listen.

They would ensure he would be heard.

A 1871 graduate of West Point, Fred Grant spent time in and out of the active military, serving in various capacities with Sherman, Sheridan, and Nelson Miles. By 1906, Fred had risen to the rank of major general in the regular army. (loc)

Grant seemed in no hurry to ink a deal. "There will be time enough to make the arrangements for publication when my book is completed," Grant wrote to Badeau shortly after Smith's visit. Contract or no, though, everyone understood that the *Century* would get Grant's memoir—a major coup for a company than had, hitherto, only published one other book.

"I am glad that you are to publish the book,"

Grant told Smith, "as I should not have written it if Mr. Johnson had not convinced me that I could."

For her part, Julia was glad for the change that came over her husband once he'd begun writing in earnest. "Happy, happy thought for him!" she exclaimed. "How many weary hours were thus occupied, and with what earnestness he began and with what perseverance he continued to the end this writing, writing, writing for bread."

* * *

A one-time theater critic from New York, Adam Badeau was assigned to Grant's staff as a military secretary in 1863 but was wounded during the battle of Port Hudson. Sent home to convalesce, he was nursed back to health by two friends from his theater circles, Edwin and John Wilkes Booth. Badeau served out the rest of the war with Grant, then served in a variety of government posts during Grant's presidency. He also had an active literary career. (loc)

To assist in his endeavors, Grant secured help from two key sources. The first was his son Fred, on hand in the Long Branch house because he'd lost his own in the collapse. He was still "looking for something to do," as he'd told reporters.

The second was Badeau, whose trusted literary eye could guide Grant's hand. Grant "said he felt inclined to write a book," Badeau later explained; "but that as my own history of his campaigns had been composed with his concurrence, and with the expectation that it would take the place of all he would have to say on the subject, he thought it right to consult me."

By that point, in early fall, the Grants had moved back to East Sixty-Sixth Street from the shore. "[T]here will be a room for you all the time you want to spend with us," Grant told Badeau. "I have taken the front room—the small one—at the head of the stairs, for my work, and converted the boudoir into a bedroom." There was also room for Badeau to work on a book of his own, a novel, that was already underway.

Grant offered Badeau fair, if not exceptionally generous, terms—he was broke, after all: $5,000 from the first 20,000 copies and $5,000 from the next 10,000.

From the start, the partnership had to have been fraught with anxiety for Badeau. His *Military History of Ulysses S. Grant* had not been a barnburner on the bestseller lists, but it was nonetheless *his*. Grant had always promised that Badeau would serve as his own last word on matters.

Grant's precarious financial situation—a change in the landscape no one had anticipated—made the memoir a necessity. Badeau knew the book would happen, with or without him. Better to

"Writing History," a sketch from Adam Badeau's *Grant In Peace*, shows Grant and Badeau hard at work as though both were writing the memoirs as equal partners. (gip)

attach himself to the project, then, in the hopes that as a collaborator of some sort he could benefit from the association. Otherwise, he could look like the odd man out, and that might kill his already tepid book sales.

I easily see Badeau's conundrum: The larger the circulation of Grant's book, the greater its importance, he lamented, and "the more completely it will supplant and stamp out mine."

Imagine that: *Help me write the book that will sink yours.*

Whatever other incentives might have motivated him, loyalty to Grant finally swayed him to sign on—but the tension would fester beneath the surface for months. "The better I help you to make [your book]," he would eventually tell Grant, "the more effectually I destroy what I have spent my life in building up—my reputation as your historian."

Opposite: A table in the editing room at Grant Cottage depicts the busy workspace of Grant's editing team—a team that would see some personnel changes between the time it first assembled on East Sixty-Sixth Street and the time it wrapped up its work on Mt. McGregor. (cm)

CHAPTER FIVE

SUMMER—FALL 1884

And that's how the story might have played out: A hoodwinked Grant rescued himself from financial destitution by the power of his pen, writing his own life story for an adoring public.

Ward made the perfect "stock villain," as his own descendant pointed out. The situation with Badeau would add to the drama as tension festered. "[A] villain he was," playwright John Guare would say of Badeau a century and a quarter later.

The book itself would be quintessentially American. "My family is American, and has been for generations, in all its branches, direct and collateral," Grant would begin. From those roots, a self-made man would rise up from obscurity under the power of his own initiative—one who would save the country and become president.

It might have all turned out that way, happy ending and everything, had it not been for the peach and all it portended. The peach transforms Grant's story from Victorian melodrama into tragedy. It has allowed storytellers for a century and a half to characterize Grant's story as heroic, noble, poignant, and sublime.

The peach starts the clock ticking.

* * *

"There was a plate of delicious peaches on the table. . . ." (cm)

The peach comes into the story on June 2, 1884, as fresh as the collapse of Grant & Ward. "It

Remembered first as a general, then as a president, Grant's legacy as a writer is often overlooked. However, said historian Bruce Catton, "All in all, Grant emerges as a man of letters of real distinction." (loc)

was during this sad summer," Julia later said, "that the fatal malady first made its appearance. . . ."

The Grants had just relocated to Long Branch but had not yet really settled in. "There was a plate of delicious peaches on the table," Julia recalled.

Grant takes one and takes a bite. It stings like fire.

Grant paces the veranda, trying to shake off the pain. It lingers. *Perhaps a doctor?* Julia suggests.

"No, it will be all right directly, and I will not have a doctor," Grant says.

Instead, he wraps his throat in a scarf. He wills it to go away. It dogs him.

For weeks, it dogs him.

Finally, his Long Branch neighbor George Childs sends his personal physician, who's in town for a housecall, over to see Grant. The doctor doesn't like what he sees, writes a prescription, recommends Grant see his own physician.

By this time, though, Grant has thrown himself into his writing. Swallowing water begins to "burn like fire," but so does the writing muse, and so he ignores the pain, marshalling his forces, pushing onward, writing, writing, writing. His own physician is in Europe, anyway. Grant will wait for his return.

This is how Grant's summer passes. Twin narratives unfold but do not yet intertwine: Grant writes his book and Grant feels increasing pain in his throat.

The burning continues.

* * *

On October 22, the nagging pain in Grant's throat at last prompted him to visit his doctor, Fordyce Barker, who had finally returned from Europe. One can easily imagine their reunion:

—*Doctor, hello!*

—*General! How are you? So good to see you!*

—*How was Europe?*

—*Wonderful! Wonderful! So what brings you by today?*

Dr. Fordyce Barker, Grant's personal physician, was on the cutting edge of the medical profession. Reportedly, he was the first American doctor to use a hypodermic needle. (gc)

One can feel the shift in the room before Grant even answers. In his clear, clean manner, he explains the problem. Barker takes a look and doesn't like what he sees. He doesn't offer a diagnosis but, instead, immediately refers Grant to an associate, Dr. John Hancock Douglas, one of the foremost throat experts in the country. That is, in itself, an answer.

Grant visited Douglas that afternoon. Grant had known the physician during the war, where he had admired Douglas's work on the battlefield.

Like Barker, Douglas examined Grant's throat. Like Barker, Douglas didn't like what he saw. Three small growths on the back of the roof of Grant's mouth, a swollen gland on the right side of tongue, an inflamed tonsil, and a tumor on the base of the tongue.

"Is it cancer?" Grant asked.

"General, the disease is serious . . ." Douglas replied. "Sometimes capable of being cured."

Later, in his diary, Douglas admitted that Grant's direct question deserved a direct response. "The question, having been asked, I could give no uncertain, hesitating reply . . . " Douglas later wrote. "I realized that if he found that I had deceived him, I could never reinstate myself in his good opinion."

"I gave him what I believed," Douglas explained, "—qualified by hope."

Douglas applied a topical anesthetic/ disinfectant and asked Grant to return twice daily for similar treatment. Grant dutifully did as he was told, riding the streetcar to the doctor's every day so that he didn't have to waste money on the extravagance of cab fair.

He didn't tell Julia about the visits. Only after she and Fred began to suspect something was up did they go to Dr. Douglas directly. He explained the situation and told the Grants that the general was likely to eventually die.

A second opinion from esteemed microbiologist Dr. George Shrady reinforced Douglas's diagnosis. Douglas provided Shrady with an anonymous tissue sample. Shrady identified it unequivocally: "This specimen comes from the throat and base of the tongue and is affected with cancer."

"Are you sure?"

"Perfectly sure," Shrady announced, adding that the patient had cancer of tongue.

"The patient is General Grant," Douglas informed him.

"Then General Grant is doomed."

"Dr. Douglas's professional qualities of leadership of the American Sanitary Commission, his various contributions to the advancement of medical knowledge during that era, and his steadfast dedication to the care of his patients represent highlights of a very honorable professional career," say researchers B. G. Bentz, E. W. Strong, G. E. Woodson, and J. P. Shah. "His final demise, bankrupt, in an ill state of health, and stripped of his professional appointment . . . seems an unjust end to the life of this notable and magnanimous laryngologist." (loc)

* * *

All the while, Grant kept writing.

"I work about four hours a day, six days a week, on my book," Grant wrote to Sherman in mid-October. He was already about a third of the way through, he added. "My idea was that it would be a volume of from four to five hundred pages. But it looks now as if it will be two volumes of nearly that number of pages each."

Grant would write, then pass the pages off to Fred and Badeau for fact-checking. The two younger men did not get along especially well—Badeau often taking a condescending tone that Fred tried his best to ignore for his father's sake. In the evenings, everyone would go over the material and lay out a plan of attack for the next day. Badeau, ever the temperamental writer, sometimes got testy, but Grant, who was used to Badeau's moody ego, ignored it.

As another part of the evening ritual, Julia joined her husband from her room, adjacent to his, to sit with him as he read to her the work he'd done that day. Fred and others often joined in. "He liked to have his pages read aloud to the family in the evening," Badeau recalled, "so that he might hear how they sounded and receive their comments." Just as importantly, he deeply appreciated Julia's devoted companionship.

"Then hope returned to me," Julia later admitted. "My husband was healthy, temperate, and strong. Why should he not be well and strong again? And down in my heart, I could not believe that God in his wisdom and mercy would take this great, wise, good man from us, to whom he was so necessary and so beloved. It could not be, and I surely thought he would recover."

Dr. George Shrady assisted on the autopsy of President James Garfield after his assassination, and he also assisted on the autopsy of Garfield's assassin, Charles Guiteau. In 1890, he would be one of the attending physicians to oversee the execution of the first man sentenced to die in the electric chair—an experience that ever after made him an opponent of that method of execution. (gc)

The Long Branch cottage came down in 1963. Today, a new generation of houses occupies the same ground. (loc)(pt)

Twain

Chapter Six

November 19, 1884

Despite his cascading white moustache, his shock of white hair, and his trademark white linen suit, Mark Twain remains one of the most colorful characters in American history.

As two of the most famous men in America, Twain and Grant not only knew each other but were friends. And on Wednesday, November 19, 1884, Twain rustled into Grant's story with the nonchalance of a man who strolls into a room and moves about without seeming to aim for any special spot, as Grant's granddaughter once suggested—although, in this instance, Twain knew exactly what he was aiming for.

Twain arrived at 3 East Sixty-Sixth to find Grant seated in the library. Nearby, Fred was paging through several sheets of paper. "Sit down and keep quiet until I sign a contract," Grant told Twain, motioning to a nearby chair. Twain sat, way back, legs crossed, chin thrown up. He had a way of occupying a chair with a morning-cup-of-coffee-and-a-newspaper air, but inside, his nerves crackled. He'd heard the night before that Grant was about to sign a contract for his memoirs, and Twain had come to talk Grant out of it.

Twain had first met Grant in 1866 and had been trying to get him to write his memoirs since 1882. Twain had initially brought up the idea during a visit he and William Dean Howells had paid Grant one early afternoon at the offices of Grant & Ward.

A statue of Mark Twain stands on the campus of Elmira College in Elmira, New York—the hometown of Twain's wife, Olivia Langdon, where the couple spent many summers. The statue, designed by sculptor Gary Weisman, weighs 376 pounds. According to the college, "From the base to the top of the structure, it is 12 feet high, which is two fathoms or, as riverboat pilots would say, mark twain." (cm)

"Mark Twain, with his . . . protruding eyebrows, which almost hid the deep-set eyes shining beneath them . . . had a vague way of striding into a room and moving about without seeming to aim for any special spot," wrote Grant's granddaughter, Julia. (loc)

Over a lunch of baked beans and coffee the idea came up and then flitted away almost as quickly. In the years since, Grant had rebuffed other offers.

"He had no confidence in his ability to write well," Twain later explained, "whereas I and everybody else in the world excepting himself are aware that he possesses an admirable literary gift and style." Grant's insights were also unique. "[W] hat another man might tell about General Grant was nothing, while what General Grant should tell about himself with his own pen was a totally different thing," Twain said.

On the evening of November 18—the night before Twain strolled into Grant's library—Twain had supped with *Century* editor Richard Watson Gilder. Gilder was expansive about the company's apparent coup: Grant was signing with them to write his memoirs based on the articles he was writing for the company's magazine. Gilder apparently thought it such a done deal that he apparently didn't mind talking about it in front of an apparent competitor.

Best remembered today as an author, Twain

published many of his own works after several unsatisfactory arrangements with other publishers. In 1884, he set up the firm Charles Webster & Company with his niece's husband, Charles—his "nephew-in-law" as Twain called him—as a one-tenth owner and the company's day-to-day manager. The company's main purpose was to publish the works of Mark Twain.

But Twain knew a sure-bet when he saw one. "[H]ere was a book that was morally bound to sell several hundred thousand copies in its first year of publication . . ." he predicted.

Now, as he sat in Grant's library, he was seeing the opportunity slip away before he even had the chance to do anything about it.

* * *

Although Grant met Twain with a passing handshake while still general in chief of the armies, their first real introduction came in 1869, early in Grant's first term as president. Twain, then a hot young literary phenom, tagged along to the White House with Nevada Senator William M. Stewart.

Grant slowly rose from his table, set down his pen, and stood "with the iron expression of a man who had not smiled for several years and was not intending to smile for another seven," Twain recalled. "He looked me steadily in the eye—mine lost confidence and fell. I had never confronted a great man before, and was in a miserable state of funk and inefficiency."

Stewart introduced them, and Twain and Grant shook—"an unsympathetic wag," Twain called it. "He did not say a word, but just stood," Twain said.

> *In my trouble I could not think of anything to say. . . . There was an awkward pause, a dreary pause, a horrible pause. Then I thought of something, and looked up into the unyielding face, and said timidly, "Mr. President, I—I am embarrassed. Are you?"*
>
> *His face broke—just a little—a wee glimmer, the momentary flicker of a summer-lightning smile, seven years ahead of time—and I was out and gone as soon as it was.*

Ten years passed before the two met again. Twain's writings had made him into a literary icon.

Grant and Twain both had roots in Missouri. Grant and his wife lived for a time with her parents at White Haven, the family plantation outside St. Louis (top). Although Grant's father, Jesse, held strong abolitionist views, Grant himself seems not to have picked them up; he married into a slaveholding family and, during his time in Missouri, he owned a single slave, whom he later emancipated. Twain, meanwhile, was born in Florida, Missouri, and grew up in Hannibal, which was some 120 miles north along the Mississippi River. Early in the Civil War, Twain served a two-week stint in a local militia unit called the Marion Rangers—an experience he recounted in his short 1885 memoir "The Private History of a Campaign That Failed." Although Twain lived in Hartford, Connecticut, by the time he and Grant entered into their publishing agreement, he never forgot his connection to the Mississippi, reflected not only in many of his writings but also even in the architecture of his New England home, which he designed to evoke the look of a steamboat (bottom). Grant's former home is now a National Park and Twain's is a privately run historic site; both locations also have adjacent museums. (bp)(jg/mthm)

Grant had served two terms in office and had just returned from his round-the-world voyage. Twain had been asked to toast the hero at a reunion of the Army of the Tennessee in Chicago.

At the kick-off of the event, Twain watched a review of the veterans from the bunting-bedecked balcony of a hotel. Suddenly, the crowd roared. Grant had appeared on the very same balcony as Twain, "looking exactly as he had looked upon that trying occasion ten years before," Twain recalled, "all iron and bronze self-possession." Before Twain could politely excuse himself, Grant approached him.

"Mr. Clemens, I am not embarrassed," Grant said, "are you?" Twain noticed the "little seven-year smile twinkled across his face again."

The time for Twain's toast came at the end of the reunion, at the end of a long, drink-soaked dinner event. Twain batted clean-up after 14 other notables—"the perilous distinction of the place of honor," Twain later said. "It was the last speech on the list, an honor no person, probably, has ever sought."

The other speakers had all lavished praise and honor and blah blah blah, so when Twain raised his glass, he took a different tack. "The Babies," he said. "As they comfort us in our sorrows, let us not forget them in our festivities."

What followed was a risky speech that took a far lighter—and some thought irreverent—tone.

After warming up the crowd, Twain pondered where the next great army commander and commander in chief would come from, just as Grant had one day been a babe himself. As a baby, Grant had no idea of the great responsibilities that awaited him in the future, during the war and in the White House; instead, he gave "his whole strategic mind . . . to trying to find out some way to get his big toe into his mouth. . . ."

The audience hung breathless at this irreverent suggestion. Twain turned to Grant, smiled, and hit his punchline: "And if the child is but the father of the man there are mighty few who will doubt that he succeeded."

Grant chortled—broke up in good-sized pieces, as Twain characterized it—and the signal released the tension of the room, which burst out in loud, enthusiastic laughter.

Twain as Grant knew him looked less like the wild white-maned lion that he's remembered as today. An 1871 photograph by Matthew Brady shows a trimmer, tamer Twain—but the askew bow-tie droops in caricature of his own bushy moustache. (loc)

* * *

Now, as Twain sat in Grant's study, it was his turn to hang suspended in silent anticipation. "I didn't know whether to laugh or cry," he later admitted.

Satisfied with the contract terms, Fred laid the contract on the table. It looked fine to him, he said. Grant rose from his chair, and taking up a pen, looked at the pages spread on the tabletop before him.

"The Stranger's Story" from the Charles Webster & Company's 1889 edition of Twain's *A Connecticut Yankee in King Arthur's Court.* In the illustration, drawn by Charles Beard, a character spins a tale of warriors and war while another listens—much as Grant did for Twain on numerous occasions. (loc)

"Don't sign it," Twain said. "Let Colonel Fred read it to me first." He'd had "a long and painful experience in book making and publishing," he added, and so might be useful to him. Grant looked at Twain, considered, then assented.

I can see Grant—his curiosity piqued—slide the document across the tabletop to Fred, who picks it up and, perhaps bemused, begins to read. Twain's bushy white moustache stands at attention as he puckers his lips and listens, his wild eyebrows drawing close in concentration.

As Fred enumerated the conditions, Twain finally interrupted. "Strike out the ten per cent and put twenty per cent in its place," he ordered. "Better still, put seventy-five percent of the net returns in its place."

Century Magazine would never go for it, Grant said, shaking his head.

There wasn't a reputable publisher in America who would not be very glad to pay 20 percent—or even 75 percent—for a book by such a colossus at Grant, Twain countered. The *Century* even expected Grant to deduct from his 10 percent "the book's share of clerk hire, house rent, sweeping out the offices," and other such "nonsense."

"They had no base intentions . . ." Twain later conceded, "but were simply making their offer out of their boundless ignorance and stupidity." The *Century* had no real experience handling books, let alone one of this magnitude.

Grant's pen remained ready to sign, but he began to waiver. Twain—charming, charismatic, and persuasive—pressed his case. For every objection Grant raised, Twain countered; however, "The General was immovable."

Fred, listening along, chimed in. This was not a

matter of sentiment, he pointed out, but rather "a matter of pure business and should be examined from that point of view alone."

Grant played the loyalty card. He'd been negotiating with the *Century*, informally and formally, for months. He did not want to be considered "a robber of a publisher."

"In that case," Twain replied, "I'm to be the publisher because I came to you first." Twain reminded Grant of the meeting, years earlier, with Dean Howells.

"Well, that's true," Grant said after a moment's consideration.

At some point during the conversation, Grant set down his pen. He was not fully persuaded, but he agreed to let the matter sit for 24 hours to mull things over. When Twain returned the next day, he went all in.

"Sell me the memoirs, General," he said. He laid out generous terms, offering a fifty-thousand-dollar advance on the spot.

We're friends, Grant said. He couldn't let Twain take such a personal risk. Sherman, after all, had made profits of $25,000 for his memoirs—far less than what Twain offered.

Twain wasn't concerned. He'd make $100,000 within six months, he was certain. If risk was the issue, then at least accept the terms he had first suggested for the *Century*, Twain said.

Friends or not, Grant still smarted from the swindling he'd suffered at Ward's hands. Rather than sign anything, he decided to seek the advice of his friend, Philadelphia newspaperman George Childs. Twain agreed that it was an excellent idea.

And away Twain swept, off on a lecture tour that would last until February. He instructed his nephew-in-law to handle the negotiations in his stead. In the meantime, Grant wrote to Childs. "Mark Twain is the company," Grant told him.

* * *

Twain, at that point, was probably the best-known literary figure in America, but Grant had another literary star show up at 3 East Sixty-Sixth that first morning of negotiations: Lew Wallace, the former army subordinate who had gone on, in

1880, to pen the wildly popular historical adventure novel *Ben-Hur*.

Wallace and Grant had skirmished with each other following a mishap at the battle of Shiloh in April of 1862. Wallace, confused by his orders and by the roads, marched his men hither and yon on the first day of battle, missing the fight entirely. Confederates, meanwhile, pummeled the rest of Grant's army, driving them nearly into the Tennessee River at Pittsburg Landing. Wallace's missing men were sorely needed. Fortunately Wallace arrived late in the day, along with Don Carlos Buell's Army of the Ohio, and the tide of battle turned on the second day.

After the war, Gen. Lew Wallace (top) penned *Ben-Hur: A Tale of the Christ*, which became the best-selling novel of the nineteenth century, surpassing the previous record holder, Harriet Beecher Stowe's *Uncle Tom's Cabin*. Only the Bible outsold it until Margaret Mitchell published *Gone With the Wind* in 1936. *Ben-Hur* was adapted for stage by 1900 and later into a movie that starred Charlton Heston. (loc)(loc)

Grant exiled Wallace for the mistake, and wide chasm existed between the two for years afterward. But by late 1884, relations between the two had begun to thaw, and evidence would soon arrive on Grant's doorstep that would modify "very materially what I have said, and what has been said by others, about the conduct of General Lew Wallace at the battle of Shiloh."

Julia, who admired Wallace's novel, played gracious hostess for Wallace as he waited for Grant. When he and Twain appeared, Julia gushed: "There's many a woman in this land would like to be in my place and tell her children that she once stood elbow to elbow between two such great authors as Mark Twain and General Wallace."

Twain ribbed Grant about the comment. "Don't look so cowed, General," he said. "You have written a book, too, and when it is published, you can hold up your head and let on to be a person of consequence yourself."

* * *

In the end, Twain got the book. They inked the deal on February 27, 1885.

"I believe the . . . company can sell a greater number than the Century," Grant concluded. "Webster offers better terms."

In fact, Twain offered terms Grant thought overly generous but which went to great lengths

Late in life, as odd-man-out reflecting on the loss of the *Memoirs*, Johnson said "it was a matter of great personal chagrin that this notable publication should not have honored the list of the Century Co. . . . The General, who knew nothing of the customs or etiquette of the publishing business, had been won over by the humorist." (loc)

to protect the general's interests. "Grant was surprised," says historian Mark Perry, "to see how far Twain was willing to go to protect the Grant family's interests rather than his own." They even went so far as to sign the legal rights for the book over to Julia, which would protect it—and its proceeds—from any of Grant's creditors.

Twain intended to sell the book by subscription: door-to-door salesmen would sell the book in advance, and when a specific number of copies were sold, Twain would finally print them. Such a practice helped publishers avoid too much up-front overhead and allowed them to print just the number of copies they'd need. But Twain knew every veteran in America—north and south—would want a copy, so he anticipated a wildly successful subscription drive.

Despite such rosy prospects, Grant declined Twain's offered advance, even though his family needed money desperately. Grant's pride would not let him take it. In the end, he would accept only a $1,000 signing bonus, which Webster sent by special courier the same afternoon the contract was signed.

"It was a shameful thing," Twain lamented, "that a man who had saved his country and its government from destruction should still be in a position where so small a sum—$1,000—could be looked upon as a godsend."

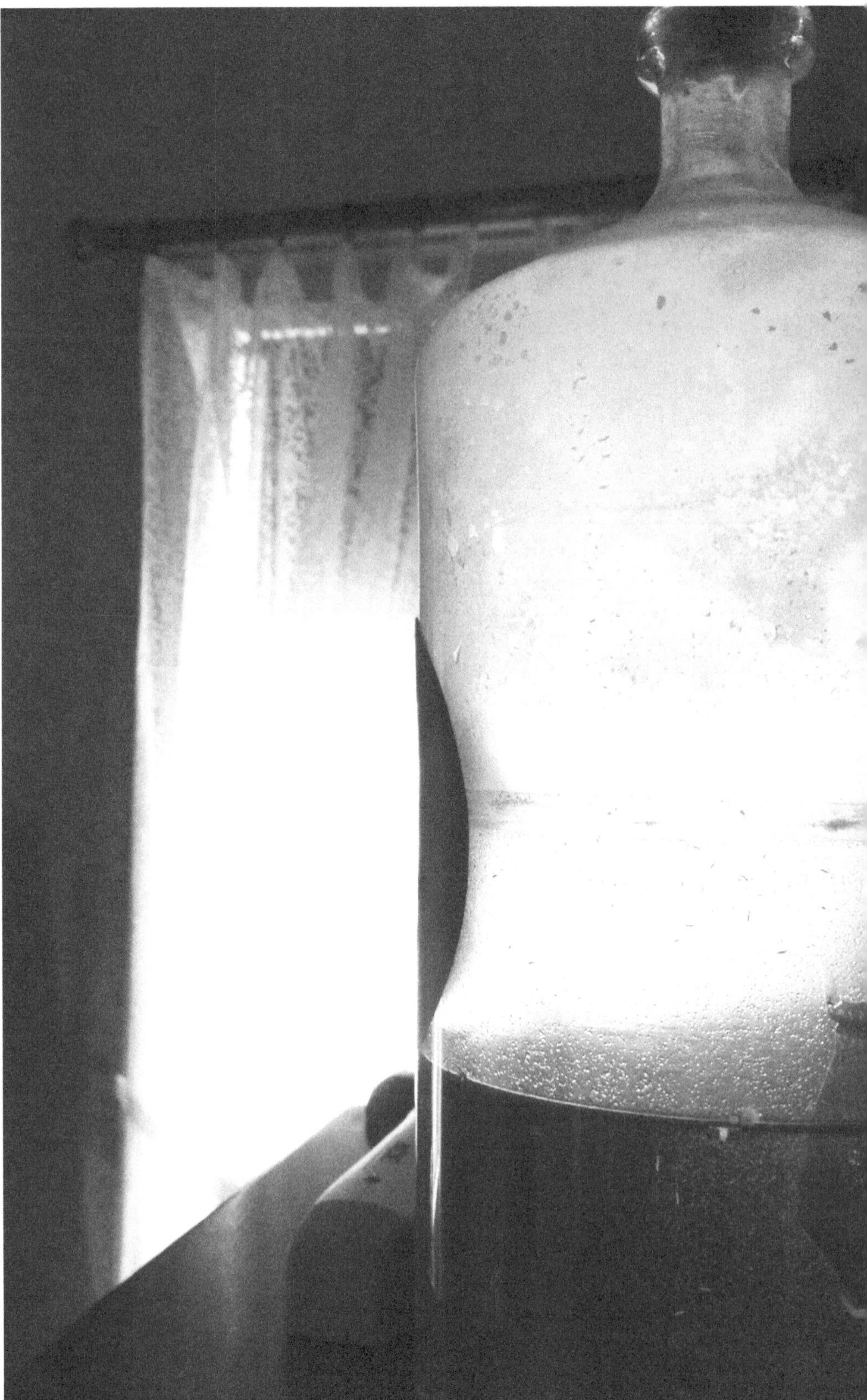

The Winter of Discontent

Chapter Seven

November—December 1884

"Gentlemen, this is the last cigar I shall ever smoke."

Grant looked sadly at the rolled tobacco in his hands. He had passed his cigar case to the small group of companions who'd joined him, and each had politely accepted.

To the east, the Hudson River valley spread out as a patchwork of browning fields and rich autumn foliage. "Blackbirds made merry . . ." said a newspaper correspondent who was with them, "and the golden sunshine filled the world about us with a wealth of autumn glories." In contrast, Grant looked "worn and somewhat haggard."

It was November 20. Grant had come to Goshen, New York, to visit the horse farm of a friend. With West Point not too far away, the visit invited reflection and nostalgia. The memoirs, too, were on his mind.

"The doctors tell me that I will never live to finish the work on which my whole energy is centered these days . . . if I do not cease indulging in these fragrant weeds," Grant said. "It is hard to give up an old and cherished friend, that has been your comforter and solace through many weary nights and days. But my unfinished work must be completed, for the sake of those that are near and dear to me."

As part of Grant's treatments, doctors swabbed his throat with a mixture of water and cocaine, intended to clean the wound and provide topical relief. Grant's original jar, with the doctors' original mixture, still stands on a cabinet in Grant's room in the cottage at Mt. McGregor. (cm)

The moment made a profound impact on the correspondent, who was now one of a small

To make himself more comfortable, Grant set up two leather chairs facing each other, which he could work and sleep in. The original chairs remain on display at Grant Cottage, although they were reupholstered in 1949 in advance of a visit to the site by Ulysses S. Grant III. (cm)

handful of people who knew anything of Grant's health problems. "[A]midst the beauty of the surroundings," the reporter said, "a sadness filled my heart that hushed my lips to silence as I contemplated the stricken hero before me slowly puffing his last cigar."

The tobacco smoke hung in the air around them like a cloud of days gone by.

* * *

Back at East Sixty-Sixth Street, work continued on the memoirs. "At this time he seemed in tolerable health," Badeau observed. "He was crippled and unable to move without crutches. . . . But he was cheerful; his children and grandchildren were a great solace to him; many friends came in to see him and to testify to their undiminshed respect." His days were devoted to his literary labor. "He worked often five, and six, and sometimes even seven hours a day, and he was not a man inclined to sedentary occupation."

Grant seldom spoke of the disgrace of Grant & Ward, but Badeau, still close to him at that point, said "those closest and dearest . . . knew that the wound was eating into his soul. This sorrow was a cancer indeed."

Aside from his closest family and inner circle, Grant had not shared news of his illness—but the illness itself refused to go unnoticed. By December, the pains had become excruciating. "[H]e could not swallow without torture," Badeau said, "and his sufferings at table were intense." At the head seat, Grant sat with head bowed over his plate, and his mouth set grimly, "his features clenched in the endeavor to conceal the expression of pain. . . ." Often, he left the meal early to pace the hall or the adjoining library in agony.

A mid-November tooth extraction went awry, adding to Grant's oral agony. "[T]he shock to the General's system was one from which he did not recover for weeks," Badeau said.

One sure source of relief to Grant's increasing pain and decreasing spirits showed up every afternoon at one o'clock: Grant's grandchildren would appear in the doorway as they passed by for lunch. They waited until he noticed them and called to them, then all would spill in and circle him. "Their prattle and kisses were always welcome . . ." said Badeau. "He took a peculiar pleasure in their society." At one point, worried that the children were disrupting Grant's work, the adults barred the children from disturbing him—but that disturbed him even more, and so he revoked their order. "They came, indeed, like a burst of light into the sick man's study, three of them, dancing, gamboling, laughing—a pretty a brood of merry, graceful grandchildren as ever a conquer claimed. . . ."

An increasingly worried Badeau noted the children provided "a delicious morsel of sweet in the midst of so much bitter care, a gleam of satisfaction in the gloom of that sad winter, with its fears, and certainties, and sorrows."

* * *

Psychologists talk of the Five Stages of Grief: denial and isolation; anger; bargaining; depression; and acceptance. They don't necessarily run in clear, neatly defined phases but sometimes overlap. Grant's stolid exterior and his family's tendency to idolize him in their reminiscences make it hard to trace the general's true emotional state, and modern historians tend to characterize Grant's struggle as heroic without considering how hopeless it might have been at times.

Grant's decision not to tell his family, to seek treatment alone in those first few weeks, might have been his attempt to isolate himself, as was his decision to hole up in the small room at the top of the stairs to write. "[M]any friends came in to see him . . ." Badeau reported, but "he never visited again."

Grant's poker face, even in the direst of emergencies on the battlefield, was famous, so it's hard now, almost a century and a half later, to see his anger. We do know, as Badeau noted, "He never relented in his bitterness to these two men," but how that manifested itself, we have no details.

Grant's focus on finishing the memoirs—if he quit smoking, maybe he could live long enough to finish his work, for instance—might be bargaining. I can see him sitting in his study, like the night under the tree at Shiloh, contemplating with grim certainty: "Lick 'em tomorrow."

All of this is lost to Grant's privacy. But one thing that does become clear, in spite of his deeply private nature, is that depression set in by December.

"If I had my health and strength, the two volumes could be completed by May," Grant wrote. "But I suffer so much with my throat that I feel no assurance of being through by that time, or even before next fall."

Worked slowed—then ceased.

"[H]is stout heart gave way," Badeau said. "All his symptoms were aggravated; his pains increased, the appalling depression of spirit returned, and more than all, the exhaustion of his strength—far greater than the disease alone could at this stage have produced."

"I have no desire to live if I'm not to recover," Grant finally admitted.

"For a while he seemed to lose, not courage, yet a little of his hope," Badeau wrote, "almost of his grip on life."

> *He had no care to write, not even to talk; he made little physical effort, and often sat for hours propped up in his chair, with his hands clasped, looking at the blank wall before him, silent, contemplating the future; not alarmed, but solemn, at the prospect of pain and disease, and only death at the end.*

It was the most appalling sight Badeau had ever witnessed: "It was like a man gazing into his open grave."

"He who had passed unscathed through Shiloh and the Wilderness," Badeau wrote, "was stricken by a weapon more fatal than the rebels ever wielded; he who had recovered from the attacks of political assailants and resisted the calumnies of partisan campaigns was succumbing under the result of the machinations of one man." (fk)

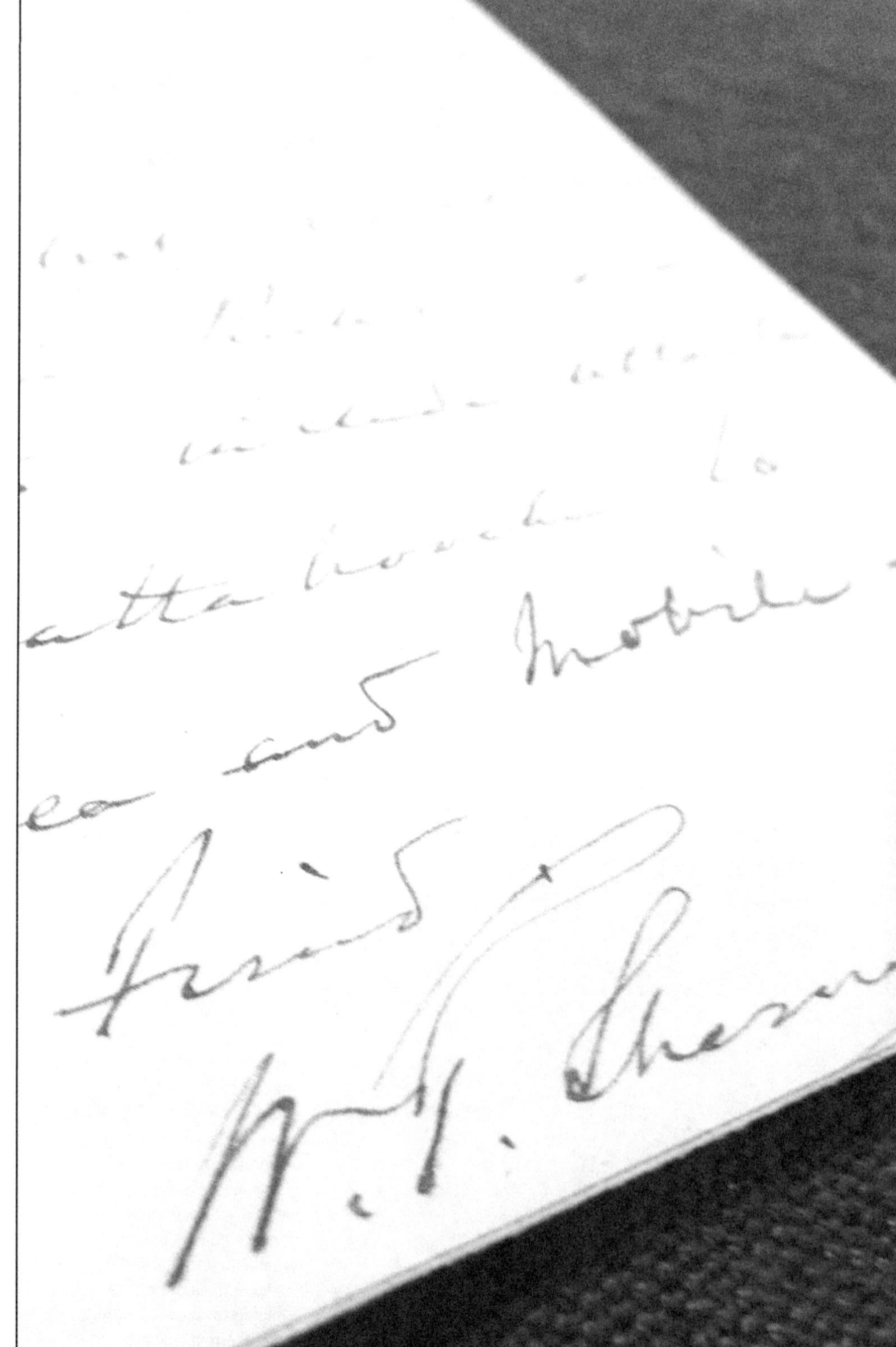

and Mobile

friend

Stage Five

CHAPTER EIGHT

DECEMBER 1884

"I am not going to commit suicide," Grant announced one day.

Badeau—concerned, dubious, relieved—tried changing the subject. Grant "cheerfully and very kindly" spoke of other things instead. That afternoon, though, he went back to work on his manuscript for the first time in days.

Julia likewise was deeply troubled by the downward spiral of her husband's spirit. One day in late December, she mentioned her concern to William T. Sherman, one of Grant's closest friends, who'd come to East Sixty-Sixth Street for two days of visiting. Sherman tried to reassure her. "But the general was always silent, Mrs. Grant," he pointed out. "Even at the worst times of strain, during the war, I used to go see him at headquarters, and he would sit perfectly still, like he did here today."

"I just walked up and down and swore then," Sherman admitted; "and I'm sure it did your husband lots of good, ma'am, and relieved his mind to have me do it for him."

Julia laughed, relieved. She'd spent enough time in the field with her husband to have seen it for herself, even if under less dire circumstances than Sherman had seen.

The relationship between Sherman and Grant was so profound that historian Charles Bracelen Flood has called it "the friendship that won the Civil War." Sherman first served under Grant at the battle

Grant's once-close subordinate, Gen. William T. Sherman, initially took the news of Grant's financial collapse hard. He had grown to believe that Grant's interactions with the moneyed class were akin to dabbling in things he shouldn't. "Look at Grant now . . ." Sherman wrote to his brother, U.S. Senator John Sherman of Ohio, on May 7. "I fear he has lost Every thing—and 'more in reputation'. . . ." (cm)

of Shiloh in April of 1862, and the two remained steadfast ever after. When Grant contemplated resigning from the army because of administrative shenanigans on the part of a superior, Sherman talked him out of it. "[S]ome happy accident might restore you to favor and your true place," Sherman told him—and indeed, Grant was soon thereafter promoted to command all troops in the West.

"We were as brothers," Sherman said of his relationship with Grant, "I, the older man in years, he the higher in rank." The implicit trust between them profoundly affected the prosecution of the Civil War. Afterwards, Sherman succeeded Grant as commanding general of the army. (loc)

Sherman played instrumental roles in Grant's campaigns for Vicksburg and Chattanooga, and when Grant was promoted to command of all Union armies in the spring of 1864, Grant promoted Sherman to take his place as commander of the Western Theater. Sherman was one of "the fittest officers for large commands I have come in contact with," Grant wrote soon thereafter. Together, their aggressive persecution of the war brought Union victory.

Most importantly, Sherman and Grant always knew the other had his back. "Grant stood by me when I was crazy, and I stood by him when he was drunk, and now we stand by each other," Sherman said, referring to bedeviling rumors that had plagued them both.

It was Christmastime, and the rangy Sherman had come to New York—a city he hated—on business. He'd heard worrisome rumors about his friend's health and had paid a visit to learn for himself. "I found Grant, Fred, and Badeau at work on his book," Sherman said. He found Grant in better shape than Fred had led him to believe, and the two old friends talked for long, long hours. "Grant says my visits have done him more good than all the doctors," Sherman wrote to his wife.

Sherman still had reason to worry about his friend by the time he took his leave. "Grant is in a bad way," he wrote to a confidant, "not so bad physically as I had been led to suppose but mentally." Financially, too, he admitted. "His business Condition is worse than I had supposed," he wrote to another.

At once, Sherman set about to establish a special fund for Grant's benefit, reaching out to some of Grant's wealthiest friends to contribute.

It took Grant only a few days to catch wind of the plan, though, and he immediately squashed it. "I appreciate both the motive and the friendship . . ."

he said, "but on mature reflection I regard it as due myself and my family to decline this generosity."

More than mature reflection might have been at work. The first check from *Century Magazine* arrived at the beginning of January—payment for Grant's Shiloh article. Grant had finally seen the fruits of his writerly endeavors. Public reaction was overwhelmingly positive. "The greeting offered to his first contribution to written history showed that the world stood ready to receive his story from himself . . ." Badeau noted, pleased.

Grant's two caretakers began to play increasingly important roles as Grant's health weakened. The first was the Grants' valet, Harrison Terrell (right), who had been with the family for three years. Terrell's role morphed into more of a nurse rather than just a valet. According to historian Charles Bracelen Flood, "Terrell understood the pain Grant increasingly felt, and how important it was to relieve it in every possible way." In March, a male nurse, Henry McSweeny (left), was added to the staff. To distinguish him from Terrell, who was mulatto, Flood says the New York Times referred to him as Grant's "white nurse." (fl)

No sooner had the *Century*'s payment come in, though, then the money went into an envelope and went right back out. "My Dear Mr. Wood," Grant wrote:

> *I take profound pleasure in enclosing to you the check which you will find with this. I wish to state to you also how great was the relief afforded by your timely loan. . . . I return you, with the greatest pleasure, one thousand dollars of the fifteen hundred which you so kindly, and without solicitation or claim upon you, sent me. It affords me greater pleasure from the fact that I have earned this by my own work.*

Grant closed by saying he hoped to send the other $500 soon. From Lansingburg, Wood tried to dismiss the remaining balance. "I will accept instead now or at any time—information that you are in good health," he wrote, "which I hope you can furnish now or speedily."

And he donated Grant's one thousand dollars to charity.

THIS FAN
GENERAL GRANT
IN JAPAN

The Greatest Showman on Earth

CHAPTER NINE

NOVEMBER 19, 1884

As the man who established "The Greatest Show on Earth," Phineas T. Barnum was probably not used to being a sideshow. He had created his spectacular traveling three-ring circus with Jumbo the Elephant as its main attraction, and he had sent the Maj. Tom Thumb—"The Smallest Person to Ever Walk Alone"—on a round-the-world tour.

"I am a showman by profession . . ." he once said, "and all the gilding shall make nothing else of me."

But the 19th century's master showman made a cameo sideshow visit in Grant's story in January of 1885. A story in the New York newspapers brought Grant's plight to Barnum's attention, and the showman responded with an ingenious idea that might take the financial pinch off the Grants.

"The whole world honors and respects you," Barnum wrote. "All are anxious that you should live happy and free from care." He alluded to Grant's financial difficulties and suggested a way for him to "achieve financial independence in an honorable manner:" Grant's collection of memorabilia from his presidency and world tour could be sent on a tour of their own as a way to raise funds for Grant.

Barnum knew a winner when he saw one. He would display Grant's articles and people would flock in droves to see them, paying a modest admission for the privilege.

Most of Grant's mementoes from his oversea trip went to paying off his debt to Vanderbilt, but this fan—still on display at Grant Cottage—survives. (cm)

Best remembered for his circus, P. T. Barnum had a career that also featured museums, America's first aquarium, "freak shows," singers, wax museums, and curiosities like the Feejee Mermaid (above). That legacy, as big as Jumbo the Elephant (right), overshadows his successful dabbling in politics as a progressive. (wiki)(loc)

Barnum offered $100,000 cash plus a portion of the proceeds, "assuming all the risk myself."

"While you would confer a great and enduring favor on your fellowmen and women by permitting them to see these trophies, you could at the same time remove existing embarrassment in a most satisfactory and honorable manner," Barnum said.

Grant invited Barnum to stop by East Sixty-Sixth to talk the matter over, but it soon became apparent that talks couldn't progress very far. The trophies were beyond Grant's control, the general feared. He had bonded them to Vanderbilt as a way to cover the $150,000 loan he owed.

Ironically, Barnum coined the phrase "Any publicity is good publicity," but Vanderbilt was being tested by that notion at the moment. Newspapers had gotten wind of his efforts to forgive the Grants' debt, but they misinterpreted his magnanimity into malice. "So many misrepresentations have appeared in regard to the loan . . ." Vanderbilt lamented in mid-January, "reflecting unjustly upon [General Grant] and myself."

Vanderbilt had cleared the mortgage on the Grants' townhouse and had repeatedly tried to forgive Grant's debt, but Grant, honor-bound, would not allow the debt to be forgiven. The loan was "an act of marked and unusual friendship," Grant said. He even went to court to force Vanderbilt to enforce the loan.

As a fortunate compromise, the Grants suggested that Vanderbilt take title to the trophies. Vanderbilt did so, but only to graciously turn the tables back on the Grants: "Now that I am at liberty to treat these things as my own, the disposition of the whole matter most in accord with my feelings is this . . .

> *[A]ll articles of historical value and interest, shall at the General's death, or if you desire it, sooner, be presented to the government at Washington, where they will remain as perpetual memorials of his fame, and the history of his time.*

One could almost hear the sigh of relief from East Sixty-Sixth Street. "In this manner you have anticipated the disposition which I had contemplated making of the articles," Grant wrote to his millionaire friend. The trophies were legally trusted to Julia to protect them from any of Grant's creditors.

Grant's honor and debt had been satisfied and, just as important, the artifacts of his legacy had been secured.

P. T. Barnum was not only one of the great showmen in American history, he was also a genius at public relations before the field ever existed, making him an important forbearer of the discipline. (loc)

Less than a year after settling with Grant, Vanderbilt would be dead. He would die on December 8, 1885, and be buried in the family mausoleum on Staten Island. (loc)

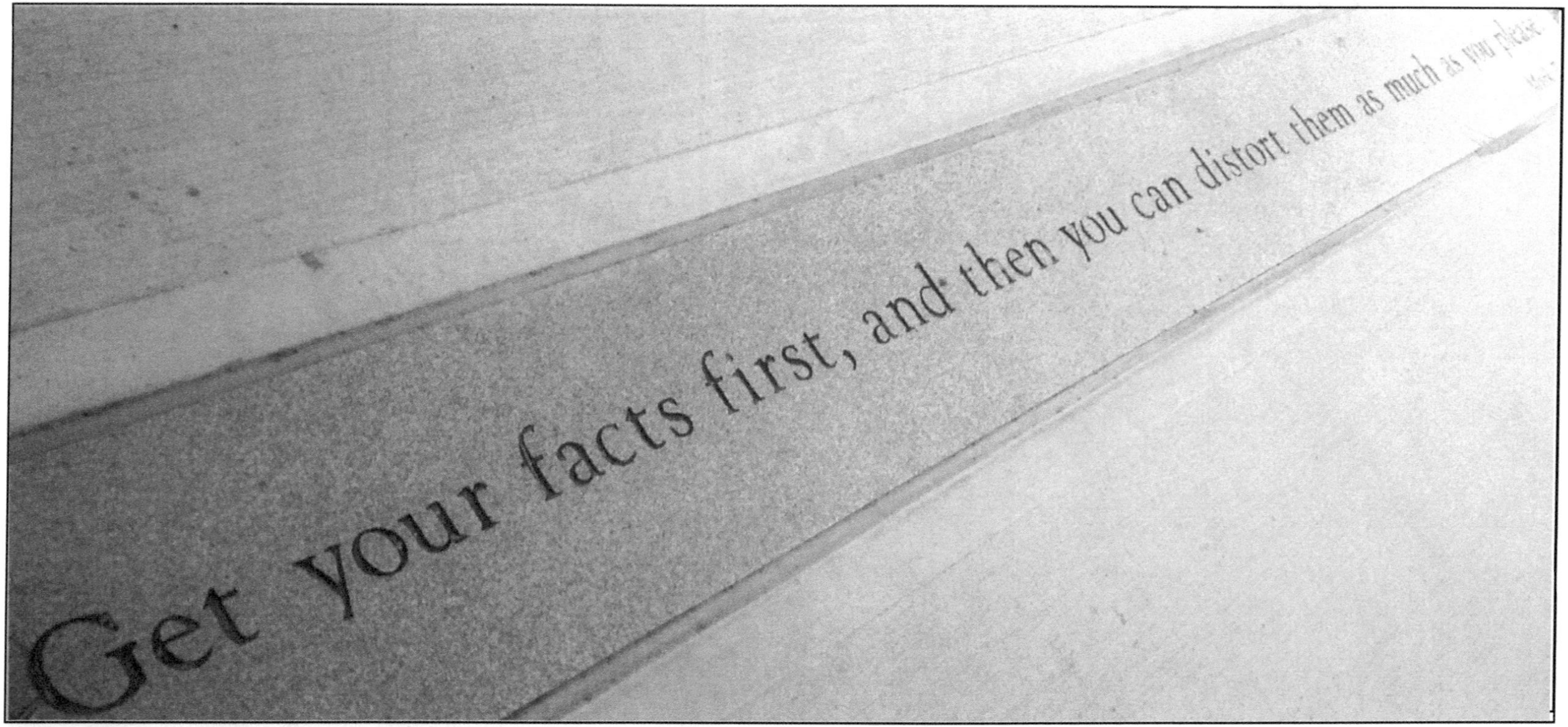

Get your facts first, and then you can distort them as much as you please.

Twain's Return

Chapter Ten

February 1885

Work continued on the memoirs. Grant finished the first volume and was partway through volume two. "He enjoyed his labors now, and quote got the literary fever for a while," Badeau said.

In mid-February, Twain returned from the speaking circuit. His nephew, Charles Webster, had kept him apprised of the book negotiations. George Childs, who'd been advising Grant, told Twain afterwards "that it was plain to be seen the General, on the score of friendship was so distinctly inclined toward me that the advice which would please him best would be the advice to turn the book over to me."

Twain swept into East Sixty-Sixth and into Grant's small room at the top of the stairs and shook hands and said he was very glad Grant was so much better.

"If only that were true," Grant replied, smiling.

Twain then learned the extent of Grant's illness. Fred, Dr. Douglas, and Grant himself all offered details. Twain seemed sobered. "I am an excessive smoker and I said to the General that some of the rest of us must take warning by his case," Twain recalled.

Twain once offered advice that could be aphoristic for memoirists: "Get your facts first, and then you can distort them as much as you please." The quote is now one of several inscribed along the sidewalk near the Mark Twain statue at Elmira College. (cm)

Douglas said the cancer had its origin in excessive smoking, but more than likely, the real reason it had manifested when it did related to "the General's distress of mind and year-long depression of spirits," arising from the failure of Grant & Ward.

Despite this grim news, such was Twain's confidence in Grant—and in the success of the project—that he still inked the book deal. "General Grant was a sick man," he later wrote, "but he wrought upon his memoirs like a well one and made steady and sure progress." On some days, Grant wrote as many as 10,000 words, working morning to night. "It kills me these days to write half of that," Twain quipped.

Selling a book door-to-door allowed a publisher to know in advance how many copies to print, thus saving money. The tactic, once common, required an army of salesmen—which Twain recruited using posters such as this one, on display at the Ulysses S. Grant Historic Site in St. Louis. (bp)

To match Grant's pace, Twain immediately kicked into high gear. He canceled a planned speaking tour of Europe and began putting into place the infrastructure he needed to print and sell the book. Twain also worked out some kinks in Grant's arrangement with the *Century* to ensure that the rights to Grant's work were free and clear.

Twain kept an eye, the whole time, on Grant's ticking clock. "He was losing valuable time because only one-half or two-thirds of the second . . . volume was as yet written," he worried. "However, he was more anxious that what was written should be *absolutely correct* than that the book should be finished in an incorrect form and then find himself unable to correct it." The constant and painstaking fact-checking cost a great deal of time, Twain said, but it was not time wasted.

"His memory was superb and nearly any other man with such a memory would have been satisfied to trust it," Twain marveled. "[W]hat a wonderful machine it was!"

Still, in an effort to speed things up, Twain encouraged Grant to bring in a stenographer, Noble Dawson, who had worked for Grant years earlier during his time in the White House.

"[H]e told me that he needed me, but he didn't want to disappoint others who needed me in Washington," Dawson recalled. "I replied that I knew no one in the Senate who would refuse to let me go if I could be of any use to him and that I would come to him immediately."

Dawson and Grant typically worked between

the hours of 10:00 in the morning and noon. In the afternoon, Grant's daughter-in-law, Elizabeth—Jesse's wife—would "read to him out of the books and refresh his memory, and he would sit with his notebook in hand and make notes." In the evening, his other daughter-in-law, Ida, would read more to him. "[H]e would sit and think and make more notes," Dawson said.

Grant never dictated at night, "as he was much too weak." Instead, Dawson worked with Fred during that time to fact-check Grant's work, huddled away in the room upstairs with the maps and notes and books. "The General had a good army library and knew where to find things," Dawson marveled.

Grant dictated "very freely and easily," Dawson said. "He made very few changes and never hemmed and hawed." One afternoon, he showed Twain the results of one of these sessions:

> *Mr. Twain was astonished when he looked at it and said that there was not one literary man in one hundred who furnished as clean a copy as Grant. The General's sentences rarely had to be revised in any way.*

Occasionally, though, Grant would direct Dawson to strike a sentence here or there. "He was always cautious in writing or talking, so as not to injure the feelings of anyone," Dawson explained, "and I remember many touching incidents of how he cut sentences which he thought might hurt someone. He was hypersensitive in this regard and often imagined things might hurt someone when they might well have been left in."

Twain noted that, too: "Even his writing looked gentle."

Twain knew he had a winner, and not just because Grant was a beloved household name. Grant's writing had style:

> *[C]larity of statement, directness, simplicity, manifest truthfulness, fairness and justice toward friend and foe alike and avoidance of flowery speech . . . . General Grant's book is a great, unique, and unapproachable literary masterpiece. There is no higher literature than these modern, simple Memoirs. Their style is flawless . . . no man can improve upon it.*

IT WAS THE GREAT HONOR OF MY LIFE TO BE PERMITTED TO BE BY HIS SIDE AND AID HIM IN THIS WORK," NOBEL DAWSON LATER SAID, CALLING GRANT "THE MOST DELIGHTFUL AND GENEROUS MAN I EVER KNEW."

Turning Back

Chapter Eleven

March 1885

The high roof of the Capitol rotunda turned the space into a vast echo chamber, and the congratulatory mood on the late morning of March 4, 1885, made the space especially loud. Senators were gathering for the inauguration of a new president, Grover Cleveland.

House members, though, were nowhere to be found. They had ensconced themselves in their chamber at the behest of former Speaker Samuel J. Randall to push through one last piece of legislation.

The bill—Senate Bill 2530—would restore Ulysses S. Grant's military pension.

The effort to restore Grant's pension dated back as far as 1881, when it was introduced to the House by former Confederate Gen. Joseph E. Johnston, then serving as a congressman from Virginia. Political opposition killed it, though, despite wide public support. "The plain fact is that [the country] was saved by him, and that, humanly speaking, this great people owes its existence, with its vast achievements and wonderful possibilities as a united nation, to him more than any one man," *The New York Times* opined.

The pension idea resurfaced with various fits and starts in the years since, and President Chester Arthur considered it a top priority, but it could never gain traction. Even the announcement of Grant's financial woes in May of 1884 did little to dislodge unsympathetic opposition.

Mementos at the Grant's Tomb visitor center offer a glance back at Grant's military career. Among the items on display is the four-star insignia of his rank as full general. Grant was the first-ever person to hold that rank in the American army. (cm)

Former House Speaker Samuel Randall of Pennsylvania and current House Speaker John Carlisle of Kentucky, both Democrats but both allies of Grant, conspired to push the pension bill forward for approval even though the clock was ticking down to the wire—and then past it. (loc)(loc)

Even this latest effort looked futile. A full and controversial agenda crowded the House's docket on its last day of business, so by the time the House adjourned on the evening of Tuesday, March 3 it had not even considered the Grant pension bill. The Constitution mandated a brief congressional recess before the inauguration of the president, so it looked as though all hope was lost. "You know during the last day of a session everything is in turmoil," Grant lamented to a friend when he heard the news of the adjournment. "Such a thing cannont possibly be passed."

But the next day, moments before noon, Randall—a Democrat, but a strong Grant supporter nonetheless—hurried into the rotunda. He began herding his Senate colleagues into their own chamber. With the parliamentary assistance of current Speaker John Carlisle, the House had reconvened, dated the final business for the day before, and shepherded the Grant pension bill through passage. Now Randall needed the Senate to do the same.

The clock ticked past noon—the traditional start-time for inauguration ceremonies—but as senators filed into the Senate, Randall directed a clerk to climb a ladder and slide the long minute hand 20 minutes backwards. Suddenly, it was only 11:40 again.

Grant's dictum "There will be no turning back" apparently did not apply on Capitol Hill.

The Senate voted. The bill passed. Grant's pension was restored. Arthur, waiting in a nearby antechamber for inauguration activities to begin, signed the bill into law as the last act of his

Capt. Isaac Bassett, an employee of the U.S. Senate for more than 60 years, turns back the hands of the Senate clock at close of a session of Congress (circa. 1892). (loc)

administration. Newly elected President Grover Cleveland officially signed Grant's commission as one of the first acts of his administration.

"The effect upon [Grant] was like raising the dead," Twain later wrote. He had been conferring with Grant, Badeau, Fred, and George Childs on East Sixty-Sixth Street when news arrived. "Hurrah! Our old commander is back!" Julia exclaimed when she heard.

The restored pension would give the Grants an annual income of $20,000, which would transfer to Julia after Grant's death. Book or not, at least her financial security was finally assured. Grant's greatest worry had been alleviated.

* * *

The vote might have been influenced, at least in part, by headlines that had begun to jump from the front pages of newspapers nationwide just a few days prior:

"Sinking Into the Grave. Gen. Grant's Friends Give Up Hope, Dying Slowly from Cancer. . . ."

The rumors that had circulated among Grant's intimates for months suddenly found legs in big, bold letters. "[T]he exact truth," Badeau confirmed, "which the family had not yet communicated in its fullness to their most intimate friends, or hardly admitted in words to themselves."

Messages of condolences, comfort, grief, and solidarity flooded Grant's mailbox. As Julia later recalled:

> *[T]he sympathy we met with from every source cannot be written: kind messages and great bouquets*

Ex-Confederates in Congress like Raleigh Colston (left) and ex-Confederates in quiet seclusion like Jefferson Davis (right) sounded support for Grant when news of his illness went public. (loc)(loc)

> *of flowers sent from the hothouses of friends, little boxes of trailing arbutus gathered from beneath the snow and set from far and wide by schoolchildren with loving messages to the General. Beautiful letters came from many schools offering prayers for his recovery, and this same prayerful petition was offered by every denomination throughout the country.*

Veterans groups passed resolutions expressing their good wishes and get-wells. "Meetings of former Confederates were held to signify their sorrow," Badeau added. "The sons of Robert E. Lee and Albert Sidney Johnston were among the first to proffer good wishes to him whom their fathers had fought."

Former Confederate President Jefferson Davis, leading a quiet retirement in Mississippi, was approached by a newsman for a reaction. "General Grant is dying," Davis responded. "Instead of seeking to disturb the quiet of his closing hours, I would, if it were in my power, contribute to his peace of mind and the comfort of his body."

Former Confederate Gen. Raleigh Colston, leading the effort among former Confederates in Congress to approve Grant's pension, wrote to Grant that he would "be gratified to know that those whom he treated generously in the day of their sorrow remember him gratefully in his hour of tribulation."

Friends and notables dropped by to pay their respects. Crowds gathered in vigil on the sidewalk in front of the brownstone. A pool of correspondents congregated, waiting for sad tidings. Scant news came from the family, though, so the reporters

As a writer and a veteran, James Grant Wilson (left) had a two-fold interest in Grant's writing project. Wilson was the son of a poet and worked as a bookseller before the war. He joined the Union army as a major, working his way up until, in 1865, he was breveted a major general. After the war, he settled in New York and became a writer and editor and, eventually, president of the Society of American Authors. He is sometimes confused with another former Civil War general, James Harrison Wilson (right), one of Grant's protégés. (loc)(loc)

began reporting gossip and arm-chair diagnosis. Grant urged his doctors—who had begun making house calls—to ignore them. "One does the work, and the other does the guessing," he said, reinforcing his support for the medical team. To make their job easier, he authorized them to make daily updates, although the updates said little.

That's not to say well-meaning well-wishers didn't try to alleviate the doctors' workload by offering all sorts of medical advice and home remedies. "[The General] pays no attention to the letters he gets in which are contained so-called 'cures,'" a members of Grant's inner circle told reporters.

All Grant wanted, particularly once the pension issue had been settled, was to get on with his writing. As the headlines reminded everyone all too vividly, he had a deadline to beat. "This was the consideration that strengthened the sinking soldier, that gave him courage to contend with fate and despair . . ." Badeau wrote.

Former Union general James Grant Wilson noted the same thing during a visit. "His mind was absorbed with the one subject of his military autobiography and a desire to be accurate in the most minute particulars," Wilson wrote. "In all matters aside from his book, Grant took but a slight and passing interest."

Events in the Senate chamber notwithstanding, the clock was ticking ever forward.

Crisis and Resurrection

CHAPTER TWELVE

LATE-MARCH—APRIL 1885

The location of Grant's greatest victory: the parlor of Wilmer McLean in Appomattox Court House, where he negotiated the surrender of Robert E. Lee and the Army of Northern Virginia. Although it was not the end of the Civil War, Appomattox did open the way for the collapse of the Confederacy. The chair on display is a reproduction; the original is on display at the Smithsonian's Museum of American History in Washington, D.C. (cm)

"Reports of my death have been greatly exaggerated," Mark Twain once reportedly said. Based on the flurry of newspaper stories from early March 1885, the same could have been said of Ulysses S. Grant.

By month's end, it nearly came to pass.

On March 26, a legal team came to 3 East Sixty-Sixth Street to take Grant's deposition in the case against James Fish and Ferdinand Ward.

"As the inquiry went on," Badeau observed, "the old spirit of battle revived; he felt all the importance of the occasion, roused himself for the effort, and made a definite declaration, damning in its evidence of the guilt of one man's action, absolute in the assertion of the purity of his own. In his testimony he spared neither Fish nor Ward; he felt that this was his last blow, and he dealt it hard."

The exertion of the effort, however, nearly killed him. Within hours, a coughing fit wracked Grant so badly that doctors had to administer a sedative.

"If you don't talk too much, you have to clear your throat," doctors told the general, encouraging him to save his strength. "It doesn't do you any good to clear your throat, so you had better not talk so much."

The next day, the coughing fit returned with a vengeance. More sedative. The next day, more coughing. More sedative.

A press pool gathered outside Grant's home, writing daily dispatches on Grant's condition. Rev. John Newman, in particular, kept them well informed as their "inside source," although the doctors also began giving daily official updates, and Harrison Terrell, on his daily errands, also gave brief, guarded remarks. (gc)

So it went until, on March 30, one of Grant's friends told reporters, "The truth is the disease has gotten away from the doctors. It is possible he may die tonight and at the very best he cannot live ten days. As he is too weak, he cannot expectorate the blood and will choke to death." Doctors admitted the next day that Grant's heart could not stand another intense coughing fit.

"All this while, the public interest was painful," Badeau reported. "So much of it penetrated into that house under the shadow of Death, that it seemed to us within as if the whole world was partaking of our sorrow."

Outside the Grants' brownstone, crowds gathered in hushed reverence—a microcosm of the world that waited in breathless silence. "Many a person between the two oceans lay hours awake, last night, listening for the booming of the fire-bells that should speak to the nation in simultaneous voice and tell it its calamity," Twain wrote.

In his cushioned chairs, Grant felt himself drowning. "If you doctors know how long a man can live under water, you can judge how long it will take me to choke when the time comes," he said to those gathered around.

Twice, as an emergency measure, Shrady and Douglas injected brandy into Grant's veins to act as a stimulant. Whether the second injection induced vomiting or it was just luck, Grant threw up a huge chunk of slime and tissue. Suddenly able to breath again, he fell asleep.

Within days, he was back on his feet, able to

Large crowds held vigil outside the Grant brownstone. "[I]t seemed to us. . ." said a member of Grant's inner circle, "as if the whole world was partaking of our sorrow." (gc)

appear at the window of his bedroom to wave weakly at the gathered throng.

"[L]ike the giant of old, he received his strength from his contact with earth," Badeau recounted with all the melodramatic flair he could muster. "[H]e rose from the embrace of the King of Terrors, and he flung himself for a while into new toils and battles, and, though wounded and bleeding, refused to die."

* * *

A frequent visitor of the time was the Rev. Dr. John Phillip Newman, a Methodist Episcopal minister who'd once served as chaplain for the U.S. Senate, where he'd become a confidant of Julia's. Newman's "sympathy and spiritual consolation was a great comfort to the General and to us all," said Julia. "The General in his big chair, with his head thrown back on the cushion, his eyes closed and his hands clasped before him, listened devoutly to the prayer of this pure and great divine."

Rev. Dr. John Phillip Newman's piousness was tinged with a Tartuffian flimflammery that made him a forerunner of the overly sincere—and often scandal-dogged—televangelists 100 years later. He constantly positioned himself as "Grant's chaplain" and courted the press in a way that made him seem an intimate part of Grant's inner circle. Grant, however, tolerated his presence for the sake of Julia's peace of mind because she admired Newman so much. (loc)

It's more likely Grant played along to ease Julia's mind. Fred later confided to Twain that Grant was "perfectly willing to have family prayers going on, or anything else that could be satisfactory to anybody, or increase anybody's comfort in any way; but he also said that while his father was . . . indeed as good as any man, Christian or otherwise, he was *not* a praying man."

Newman pops up as a mildly roguish figure disguised in sheep's clothing. Well-meaning and generally harmless, he nonetheless used his influence with Julia to jockey for a favored position, wanting to be seen as "Grant's pastor" during the general's last days. He made an effort every day to speak to the press, putting words in Grant's mouth as he recounted events from inside the Grant household.

"Some of the speeches he put into General Grant's mouth were to the last degree incredible to people who knew the General," Twain groused, "since they were such gaudy and flowery misrepresentations of that plain-spoken man's utterances. . . . General Grant never used flowers of speech, and dead or alive he never would have uttered anything like that."

On multiple occasions, Newman tried to seek deathbed conversions from Grant. "I would only be too happy to do so if I felt myself fully worthy . . ." Grant once cagily replied, but "no worse sin can be committed than to take [communion] unworthily. I would prefer therefore not to take it, but to have the funeral services performed when I am gone."

* * *

Grant's resurrection came just days before Easter. Days after that, he had occasion to light up a cigar—his assertion at the horse farm back in November notwithstanding.

April 9 marked the 20th anniversary of Robert E. Lee's surrender at Appomattox Court House. "One of the sons had a presentiment that his father would not survive that day," Badeau recalled; "but it would have been hard to have General Grant surrender on the anniversary of his greatest victory."

A new wave of letters and notes poured in from friends, well-wishers, dignitaries, and veterans. For days, the messages came. "I receive a hundred letters

It was hardly an imaginative leap or a bold assessment, but the November 14, 1868, edition of *Harper's* credited Grant's victory in the presidential race to his victory over the Confederacy. (loc)

in a mail and several mails a day," an overwhelmed but grateful Grant told a reporter.

Typical was a note from the soldiers and sailors of Northern Ohio, assembled in Cleveland to celebrate the anniversary. "[W]ith hearts surcharged with the tenderest affection for their old commander, which the lapse of 20 years has only served to strengthen and intensify," they wrote, "[we] send to you their most sincere sympathy in this hour of your great physical suffering. With admiration and love for you as a soldier and as the first citizen of the Republic, which only broadens and deepens as time passes, we tender a soldiers' greeting and God bless you."

From Michigan came an especially touching note:

> *I am a little girl and have never been to school but do my lessons at home with mama. My reader is*

> *Harpers Young People and this morning I read such a nice story about you. I went down to the news-room to buy a copy to send to you but they were all gone so mama said I might write and tell you and if you could not read it your self perhaps some of the kind people who are with you would read it to you. My papa was a soldier and loves you very much but he is a lawyer now and does not fight any more, though mama says he often fights his old battles over again. He is commander of the [GAR] post and last week . . . everybody made speeches about General Lee's surrender to General Grant. . . .*
>
> *I shall send you a Birthday card and it will be a truely [sic] present from me. I shall buy it with the money that I have earned. Mama says it is not a real present if you ask papa for the money to buy it with[.] I shall put my name on it so you will know it is from me for I suppose you will get a great many.*
>
> *Good bye, dear General Grant. I love you very much and wish I could do something to make you well.*

Grant's birthday came on April 27. Andrew Carnegie sent 63 roses—one for each of Grant's years. Friends stopped to visit. A larger-than-usual crowd clustered outside. More letters came. In Topeka, Kansas, 20,000 people assembled for a huge birthday celebration in Grant's honor.

"The dispatches have been so numerous and so touching in tone that it would have been impossible to answer them if I had been in perfect health," Grant said.

Again, as had happened in May in the wake of the failure of Grant & Ward, Grant's health crisis in late March was countered by an outpouring of support that helped sustain him.

* * *

"The public only know of but a fraction of the expressions of sympathy which I have received," Grant admitted to a reporter.

All eyes were on Grant by this time. He had lived in open view for more than two decades, so he was used to the public eye being on him. But imagine *all* eyes—hypnotized by his pendulous condition.

From the headline "Grant is Dying" that screamed for attention to his real brush with death, from the congressional reinstatement of his pension to the grand celebrations of his greatest victory—instance after instance, public attention focused on him again and again. Imagine a national birthday celebration while also knowing it was likely your last.

"My chances, I think, of pulling through this are one in a hundred," he predicted.

Behind the scenes, the great hero of the age was still withering, still suffering. Dr. Shrady recalled a quieter incident from late that month that reminds us of Grant's fragile humanity.

One night, intense pain wracked the patient so badly that he called for Shrady for something, anything, that would help. Shrady, worried about over-medicating Grant with too many narcotics, offered soothing words instead.

"Just imagine you are a boy again," the doctor suggested. "Curl up your legs, lie over on your side, and try to doze off, as you used to do in days gone by."

Puck painted a picture of the Young Napoleon in exile—although Ferdinand Ward went to Sing Sing prison, not the Isle of Elba. He served six and a half years of a ten-year sentence. James Fish, sent to the prison in Auburn, New York, served four years of seven. Grant later said of Fish, "He was not as bad as the other." (loc)

Grant seemed pleased by the idea and complied.

"Put your hand under the bolster and rest your head on it," Shrady continued softly; "bend your knees a little higher, curl forward more, There you are. Now I shall tuck you in. Now go to sleep like a boy."

Within minutes, Grant slept soundly. As the doctor withdrew from the bedside, he found Julia standing in the doorway, watching the entire scene. Sheepishly, Shrady tried to apologize. "I don't know how the General will like that kind of treatment," he said. "He may think it inconsistent with his dignity to be treated like a child and may not understand the real motive."

"No danger of that," Julia replied. "He is the most simple-mannered and natural person in the world, and he likes to have persons, whom he knows, to treat him without ceremony."

Bad "Water," Bad Blood

CHAPTER THIRTEEN

APRIL 29, 1885

Twain was delighted by Grant's ongoing output, not only because he continued to make such solid progress toward finishing the manuscript but also because of the book's surprisingly high quality. "The fact remains and cannot be dislodged that General Grant's book is a great, unique and unapproachable literary masterpiece," Twain declared. "There is no higher literature than these modest, simple Memoirs. Their style is at least flawless, and no man can improve upon it."

Twain mentioned to Grant that he'd been comparing the memoirs to Caesar's Commentaries. "I was able to say in all sincerity that the same high merits distinguished both books—clarity of statement, directness, simplicity, manifest truthfulness, fairness and justice toward friend and foe alike and avoidance of flowery speech. General Grant was just a man, just a human being, just an author. . . ."

Unfortunately, the comparison to Caesar would extend beyond the book. With pen in hand poised as a dagger, Grant's own Brutus was about to stab him in the back.

* * *

As a self-styled member of the literati, Adam Badeau saw himself on equal authorship footing with Grant. (cm)

On April 29, one of the New York newspapers, still looking for a story, decided to invent one. It reported that Adam Badeau, not Grant, was the

The political cartoonist who depicted Grant as Caesar was not the first to make the comparison. Grant was often lauded as a military leader on par with the greatest of all time. (loc)

author of Grant's memoirs. "The most the general has done upon the book has been to prepare the rough notes and memoranda for its various chapters," the paper said.

The imperturbable Grant suddenly found himself deeply perturbed.

"The composition is entirely my own," he stated categorically. Twain, less eloquently, threatened legal action.

Badeau remained silent.

Publicly, at any rate—but later that day, Badeau materialized at Grant's side, passed him a note, bowed, and exited.

The note outlined a list of grievances and demands. Aside from the financial arrangement the two had already reached, Badeau now wanted an additional $1,000 a month to finish the book, plus 10 percent of the overall profits from the book. In exchange, Badeau would "declare as I have always done that you wrote it absolutely."

Et tu, Badeau?

Unfortunately for Brutus, this was not the Ulysses S. Grant who had wanted to withhold his final articles to the *Century* until he first received Badeau's approval. Grant had found his voice as a writer, and he knew he had something worthwhile to say. He had been praised by Twain, a renowned writer and good friend he admired deeply and whose opinion he valued. He'd been enthusiastically received by Johnson and the staff at the *Century*, whose opinion he'd likewise respected.

Badeau's note smacked of blackmail, but Grant didn't even blink. "[Y]ou and I must part all association so far as the preparation of any work goes which is to bear my signature . . ." he wrote in reply. "My name goes to the book and I want it so in the fullest sense." He dismissed Badeau's terms as "preposterous."

Just as part of Badeau's letter enumerated an array of grievances about the book, Grant's reply enumerated an array of observations about Badeau. "You are petulant, your anger is easily aroused and you are overbearing even to me at times," Grant said.

Just as Grant's memoirs told it as he saw it, so did his letter to Badeau. The shots came like cannonballs crashing through a forest, with Grant sitting amidst the cacophony, calmly writing.

The man who once said "Let us have peace" did ended his candid letter on a magnanimous note, though: "You can always be the welcome visitor at my house that you have been before." He signed it, "Your friend and well wisher."

Badeau moved out.

* * *

Badeau's treason would stick sharply in Grant's craw for the few months left to him. As a soldier and politician, Grant had valued loyalty above all things. This betrayal from one of his closest aides—a man Grant had done so much for—must have burned especially bad in the wake of Ward's betrayal.

In mid-July, Grant would write to Badeau one last time. "I have thought very much about you and your affairs," Grant wrote. "It is not possible now that I can be of further assistance to you. My health and other circumstances prohibits it." While his health was, indeed, an issue, Grant suggested that it might just be an excuse. "I was thinking . . . of what I had done for you for the last twenty years and could not do again if I would," Grant admitted. "To be frank with you, you are helpless, and filled with a false pride."

Grant laid out several examples of Badeau's surly temperament and condescending attitude, then offered some advice "in the best of spirit:"

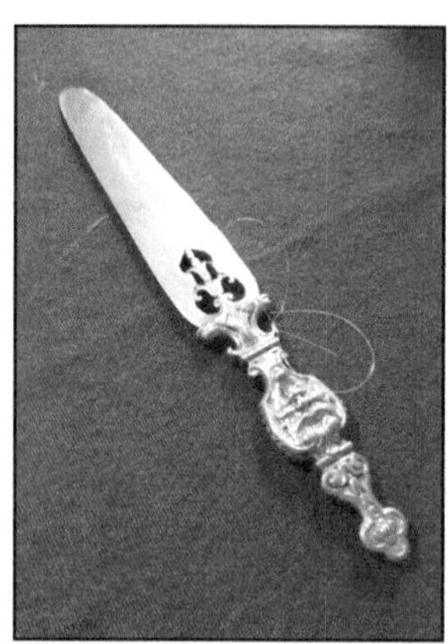

A letter opener on display at Grant Cottage looks more like something Badeau might have used for his back stabbing. (cm)

> *[L]ook upon yourself for a while as you have heretofore looked upon others. Take up you[r] pen and go to work earnestly. Regard yourself as belonging to the publisher who pays you for your work, for the time being, and not upon him as being "My publisher." You make the offensive ownership apply to the other man always.*

Grant pointed out that pages of the *Memoirs* Badeau had copyedited and fact-checked "gave more trouble than all the balance."

"The more I have thought of what took place just before you left my house the more strongly convinced I become that your nature is not of that unselfish kind I had supposed," Grant concluded. "I am also satisfied that my book would never have been finished as 'my book' if you had been permitted to continue in the capacity you now seem disposed to think you were in. I however never regarded you in any such capacity."

With all of that off his chest, Grant scribbled a note at the bottom: He didn't want the letter sent but, rather, kept as an ace up the sleeve should his family ever need it.

* * *

In the end, Badeau would get the last word—ironically as a result of the very thing Grant suggested in his unsent letter. In 1887, Badeau would publish *Grant in Peace: From Appomattox to Mt. McGregor*, a 633-page account of Grant's presidency, trip around the world, and final days.

The book brims with swollen purple prose: "He who had passed unscathed through Shiloh and the Wilderness was stricken by a weapon more fatal than the rebels ever wielded; he who had recovered from the attacks of political assailants and resisted the calumnies of partisan campaigns was succumbing under the result of the machinations of one man."

Badeau conveniently omitted any references to his own machinations and his subsequent fallout with Grant. Instead, he takes the tone throughout of an intimate insider, and after his banishment, he merely brushes aside his absence by excusing himself from the scene: "I was not with him at Mount McGregor. . . ."

It's possible to read the book and wonder whether its fawning tone was Badeau's honest attempt to do right by his commander in the end. It's also possible to interpret his tone as a calculated attempt at reverence designed for commercial appeal.

Grant in Peace drew the curiosity of readers because it covered events Grant did not himself cover in the *Memoirs*, but by and large, the public looked at Badeau as someone trying to capitalize on Grant's death to make a quick buck, harassing Julia and the rest of the family in the process. He further tarnished his image by suing for the money he said Grant had promised him out of the *Memoir*'s royalties.

In 1888, Julia would finally settle for $11,254.97, while Badeau had to publicly state that Grant had been the sole author and Badeau's role was limited to "suggestion, revision, and verification." In the end, Badeau got exactly what Grant had promised him.

It was not the happy ending he had tried to connive.

The Final March

CHAPTER FOURTEEN

LATE MAY—MID-JUNE 1885

Grant stood in the window and watched them pass: the proud veterans of the Grand Army of the Republic. Rows upon rows of the former soldiers, unit after unit. They dipped their scarred battle flags in salute as they passed by Grant's window.

Bands played. Crowds cheered. Hooves clopped on the street.

It was Decoration Day, May 30, and the parade had made its way straight down Fifth Avenue. The route of march this year, however, had veered from its usual path and detoured along East Sixty-Sixth Street, past the brownstone at number 3.

Grant had been suffering a particularly bad day, but at the sound of his former men, he arose and dragged himself to the window, recalled his friend and most trusted former aide, Horace Porter. Grant's eyes kindled once more with flame.

The veterans returned his gaze. "[I]n spite of military discipline, all eyes turned upward," Grant's granddaughter remembered, "and they gazed at the fine strength of that face, still fighting and unconquered."

For Porter, standing with his old friend and commander, it was a poignant moment. "[T]hose war-scarred veterans with uncovered heads and upturned faces for the last time looked upon the pallid features of their old chief," he wrote. "[C]heeks which had been bronzed by Southern suns

As Grant's voice began to fail him, he took to conversing with people by writing on slips of paper. Samples of his "pencil talk" are now mounted on display at Grant Cottage. (cm)

and begrimed with powder, were bathed in tears of manly grief."

Grant had watched the army pass in grand review on May 23 and May 24, 1865, at the war's close. In the years since, he'd watched armies of veterans march in other reviews, including the year before when he'd traveled to Brooklyn for Decoration Day with Phil Sheridan. But this—this, he knew, would be his last review.

Grant "slowly and painfully" raised his hand in salute. A hush fell over the crowd. The army passed. Grant watched them go, knowing he was soon leaving them.

It was Grant's last military salute.

* * *

The veterans were much on Grant's mind. They had sustained him after his financial collapse, and they had convinced him he had something about the war worth saying, prompting his writing career.

On May 23, Grant decided to pay them the highest honor he could think of. "These volumes are dedicated to the American soldier and sailor," he wrote in his manuscript.

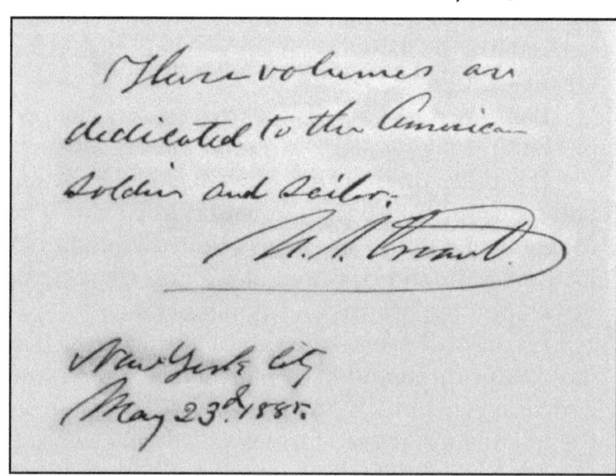
These volumes are dedicated to the American soldier and sailor.
U. S. Grant
New York City
May 23d 1885.

While Grant never wanted people to forget that the Civil War was fought to reunify the country, the dedication of his book to all soldiers stood as a marked example of the reconciliationist spirit that touched veterans of both sides. (cm)

Fred, perplexed when he saw the addition, suggested his father specify "soldiers of the North."

"It is a great deal better that it should be dedicated as it is," Grant assured him. "The troops engaged on both sides are yet living. As it is the dedication is to those we fought against as well as those we fought with. It may serve a purpose in restoring harmony."

* * *

Grant finally took his leave on June 16. Doctors had feared that the onset of summer heat would prove deadly to their patient and so had scoped out a cooler environment. With any luck, a milder climate would let him live into the autumn.

Left: With Douglas standing nearby, Grant bid adieu to the large crowd that had gathered outside his home to see him off. Below: Terrell helped Grant climb aboard the carriage that would take him to the train station. (gc)(fl)

The doctors' choice: a mountaintop retreat just nine miles outside Saratoga, New York, which itself was 180 miles north of the city. Grant's friend, industrialist Joseph Drexel, owned a small summer home on the mountaintop, Mt. McGregor, near a new luxury hotel, the Balmoral. Drexel insisted Grant make use of the cottage and even had the place quickly renovated to better suit Grant's stay.

To get to Mt. McGregor, Grant boarded a special train made available to him by his ever-magnanimous friend, William Vanderbilt. The entourage included Julia; their daughter, Nellie; Fred and his wife, Ida, and son and daughter, plus their nanny; their youngest son, Jesse, and his wife, Elizabeth; Dr. Douglas; Grant's manservant, Harrison Terrell; Grant's nurse, Henry McSweeny; and stenographer Nobel Dawson. Dr. George Shrady traveled along for part of the way to his own summer home in nearby Kingston. Staff members from the Balmoral Hotel and a press pool from the New York City papers rounded out the assemblage.

The train ride north from New York to Saratoga was stifling hot, but the air cooled a bit as the party ascended Mt. McGregor. (gc)

Up the Hudson River Valley, the train chugged. They passed West Point, where Grant had been a cadet some 42 years earlier. They passed Goshen, where Grant had smoked his last cigar the previous November. They passed Albany, the state capital. "At station after station on the route knots of people were waiting to wave greeting and godsend," one reporter wrote.

Despite the throngs of well-wishers, the trip could not have been pleasant. Temperatures soared past 100, forcing everyone to open theirs windows for any kind of cooling breeze—but that also brought smoke and cinders from the locomotive. Grant, facing the caboose to protect himself from the flecks of ash as much as possible, tried to doze.

Joseph Drexel, the son of the founder of Drexel University, spent most of his adult life as a philanthropist after tiring of the cut-throat banking business that had been his family's legacy. (gc)

At one point along the way, the train was diverted to a side track at one of the stations. A rail yard operator, about to throw the switch to send the general's train back on its way, saw Grant sitting in his car. Well within speaking distance, the railman hailed his former chief: "General, it is good to see you alive!"

Grant acknowledged him, then watched as the man, with great difficulty, threw the switch. Only then did Grant notice the railman had only one arm. Grant indicated the missing limb.

"General," the man said, "I lost my arm in the Wilderness. And I would gladly give up my other one for you if it could somehow make you well again."

The train rolled away through a billow of steam and smoke before Grant could respond.

* * *

The train arrived in Saratoga some six hours after departing Manhattan. There, Grant's party had to switch trains for the steep, twisting route up the mountainside. Grant's leather chairs proved a particular challenge to transfer, their size and bulk and sweat-slippery surface making them hard to manhandle. With cane in hand, the general directed the action.

As at other stations, a crowd had amassed to greet the general. Initially, he was also supposed to inspect the members of the local GAR post, which had assembled in formation along the train platform. Grant's weakened condition alarmed his former men, though, and they called off the review so as not to tire him further. Grant nonetheless raised his cane to them in salute.

TOP: The view of Mt. McGregor today from the valley below. The prison is visible along the left of the mountaintop. An indentation in the trees about a quarter of the way from the right-hand edge of the page reveals the location of Grant Cottage. The gash in the trees on the photo's right edge is the eastern overlook.
BOTTOM: A historic view of Mt. McGregor shows the Balmoral Hotel perched atop the mountain. (cm)(gc)

The "12-mile jolt" up the mountainside took less than an hour. At the top, a painted wooden sign hung over the wooden boardwalk from the rail platform to the Balmoral: "Welcome to Our Hero." Grant carefully climbed down from the train and, refusing help, began to make his way up the path toward the Drexel's cottage. He soon tired, though. Halfway up the sloping path, two local police officers scooped him into a wicker chair and carried him the rest of the way.

Grant refused to stay down, though. Inside the

cottage, Harrison Terrell brushed the locomotive ashes from his beard. With Terrell's help, Grant put on a black coat and his top hat, then the two men stepped outside to see just what this new place was all about, anyway.

The train station at the top of the mountain stood not far from the Drexel cottage where Grant stayed. (gc)

The wide, wooden porch wrapped around three sides of the building. One can almost hear Grant's footsteps, quiet in their shuffling, complimented by the hollow *thunk* of his cane as he paced the porch's length. Birdsong filled the mountaintop trees. The Balmoral Hotel loomed at the crest of the mountain, and the Hudson Valley spread out wide and beautiful to the east.

This was it, Grant knew: This was the place he'd come to finish his work. And this was the place he'd come to die.

* * *

During this time, Grant's cancer-choked voice finally gave out for good.

The promenade from the station to the hotel offered a "Welcome to Our Hero."(gc)

"As he went on his voice became weaker and weaker, and toward the last, I had to take my seat very close to his, and he whispered his words in my ear while I took them down in shorthand," recalled Nobel Dawson. "The dictation for him was painful and his voice got lower and lower as he went on. At last, it was a mere whisper. . . ."

Grant could croak in a barely audible whisper—louder if he had to—but as he told Dr. Douglas, he kept as quiet as possible in order to preserve his strength until, finally, he gave up speaking almost entirely.

"It is just a week to-day since I have spoken," he wrote on June 18 to Rev. Newman.

Instead, he took to writing on slips of paper to hold up his end of any conversation. People called it Grant's "pencil-talk." "[H]e used a yellow manila legal pad with blue lines and he wrote with a pencil," Dawson explained. "The work tired him very much, and at the end, he was only able to scratch down his ideas."

When the end finally seemed imminent, Fred ordered "all manuscripts and literary effects at the cottage office . . . be at once packed up and made safe." As part of this effort, Dawson would collect as many of the slips of pencil-talk as he could and give them to Fred and Julia for safekeeping. "This was doubtless a hardship at the moment, but was fortunate in the end for his fame," reflected Badeau, who was no longer with the general by this time, "for the sentences jotted down from time to time were preserved exactly as they were written, and many of them are significant."

A historic map shows the twisting route up the mountain from Saratoga. Rising 1,200 feet above sea level, Mt. McGregor got its name from local lumberman Duncan McGregor, who owned a thousand acres of the mountain, including its summit. (gc)

I find it one of the story's great ironies: Even as Grant finally found his voice as a writer, he lost his literal voice.

So once again his writing saved him. He would not go quietly into that good night. He would write and write and write—if not on his memoirs then in conversation, instruction, and request.

He might be short of voice but never for words.

* * *

"My dear wife," Grant wrote to Julia a few days later: "There are some matters which I would like to talk but about which I cannot. The subject would be painful to you and the children, and, by reflex, painful to me also. When I see you and them depressed I join in the feeling."

Grant and Douglas (gc)

> *I have known for a long time that my end was approaching with certainty. . . . I had an idea, however, that I would live until fall or the early part of winter. I see now, however, that the time is approaching much more rapidly.*

In the letter, Grant discussed his wishes for burial. He knew the matter would, in all likelihood, become a matter of public spectacle. Whatever

As one of the owners of the Balmoral Hotel, banker and philanthropist Joseph Drexel bought a vacant cottage on the top of Mt. McGregor to use as a summer home. He never occupied the cottage, though, offering it instead to Grant for his use. Drexel later preserved the house as a shrine and memorial in Grant's honor. (cm)

the final result—West Point; Washington, D.C.; a plot they owned in St. Louis; New York where they made their home late in life—what mattered most was that there be room for her to join him when the time came: "I hope far in the future," he added.

He left with Fred a memorandum that outlined the disposition of his book proceeds. But it was to Julia that the most important task would fall: "Look after our dear children and direct them in the paths of rectitude. It would distress me . . . to think that

The Drexel cottage sat just downhill from the Balmoral Hotel (top). Built in 1881, the hotel opened seasonally to accommodate guests in 300 rooms. Serviced by its own narrow-gauge rail service, it also boasted its own private generator. The hotel, four stories tall, also boasted wide promenades for fresh air and stunning views (bottom). (gc)(gc)

one of them could depart from an honorable, upright and virtuous life. . . ."

When he finished, Grant tucked the letter in his coat pocket, along with a ring Julia had given him, and locks of her hair and Buck's hair. He wrote: "This will be found in my coat after my demise."

Chapter Fifteen

Mid-June—Mid-July 1885

Five days after arriving at Mt. McGregor, Grant resumed work on his memoirs. Twain was sending him printed proofs of volume one for review, and Fred and Noble Dawson reviewed with him the nearly completed handwritten manuscript for volume two. Grant worked several hours each morning, dictating to Dawson in a whisper, making corrections to both volumes, working as feverishly as his deteriorating condition allowed.

"There is much more that I could do if I was a well man," he told Twain on June 29. "I do not write quite as clearly as I could if well. If I could read it over myself many little matters of anecdote and incident would suggest themselves to me."

The lethargy clung to him. "I am very thankful I have been spared this long because it has enabled me to practically complete the work in which I take so much interest," he told Dr. Douglas on July 2, but he bemoaned his lack of energy. "I can not stir up strength enough to review it and make additions and subtractions that would suggest themselves to me and are not likely to to anyone else."

By July 5, though, Grant caught another wind. "I had begun to feel that the work of getting my book to-gether was making but slow progress," he admitted to Douglas.

> *I find it about completed, and the work now to be done is mostly after it gets back in gallies. It*

Visitors to Grant Cottage today enter a room originally intended as Julia's living space, but she didn't like it, so it soon became the work space for Grant's fact-checkers, primarily Fred and Dawson. Modern displays suggest the writing, editing, and revision that took place there, with ample lighting from two windows to facilitate the work. (cm)

can be sent to the printer faster than he is ready for it. There [are] from one hundred and fifty to two hundred pages more of it than I intended. Will not cut out any thing of interest. It is possible we may find a little repetition. The whole of that is not likely to amount to many pages. Then too there is more likelyhood of omissions.

He also added a 550-word preface to the first volume. "I would have more hope of satisfying the expectation of the public if I could have allowed myself more time," Grant wrote. He was, of course, under the ultimate deadline.

"Man proposes," he admitted, "and God disposes."

* * *

Bath chairs got their name from the English seaside town of Bath, where they were first widely used. This one sits on display at the Grant Cottage visitor center. (cm)

To ensure Grant got the privacy he needed for work and rest, a local veteran took it upon himself to set up camp outside the cottage and stand guard. Sam Willett had been 45 years old when he enlisted in 1863 in Company A of the Sixteenth New York Heavy Artillery. After the war, he went back to work as a shoemaker in Albany. When Willett heard of Grant's pending arrival at the Drexel cottage, he set up an old army tent not far from the southeast corner of the cottage, furnished the tent with a

Sam Willett, 65, proudly volunteered into service for his old commander, acting as unofficial gatekeeper. He was a favorite of Grant's grandchildren, who played in his tent and often enlisted him to push them on a swing. (gc)

woodstove and washtub, put on his GAR uniform, and prepared for sentry duty.

Move along, move along, he would tell sightseers intent on catching a glimpse of Grant.

Grant sometimes looked up from his manuscript or his newspaper and acknowledged the visitors, but more often than not, he was content to let Willett handle the traffic.

The family, meanwhile, settled into a routine that included meals in a private dining room at the Balmoral. Grant would ride up the hill in a special Bath chair delivered to the mountain at Douglas's request. Willett would stand guard, although the grandchildren frequently invaded his space and made off with him when things were otherwise quiet. Grant would sit in his wicker chair on the porch and read the newspaper and work on his book.

"The fact is that I am a verb instead of a personal pronoun," Grant observed one day. "A verb is any thing that signifies to be, to do, or to suffer. I signify all three."

* * *

By day's end, Grant's throat needed the attentions of Dr. Douglas. Douglas would swab Grant's mouth, clearing away mucus and tissue. He applied cocaine water from a tall glass apothecary jar that sat atop a cabinet in Grant's office/bedroom. "[T]aken properly, it gives a wonderfull amount of relief from pain. . . . " Grant said.

But the cocaine addled his mind, too. "I had something that I wanted to write and can do that better in bed with my table before me," he told

By evening, Grant needed the ministrations of his doctors and TLC from his family. (fl)

Grant's room in the cottage was (and still is) dominated by his face-to-face chairs (right). A cabinet of his personal belongings, offering a glimpse into his day-to-day life, stands along one wall (below). (gc)(cm)

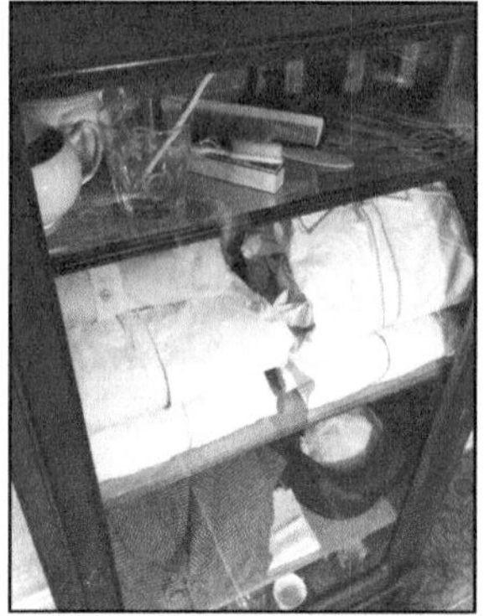

According to one popular bit of hearsay, the Federal Drug Enforcement Agency comes to Grant Cottage once a year to measure the amount of cocaine water in the glass jar that still sits on the cabinet in Grant's room. It's just a myth, however. (cm)

Fred. "I went to sleep and now forget what it is that I want to write about."

Even worse, he could feel the cocaine's addictive effects beckoning to him. "When the medicine is being applied the tendency is to take more than there is any necessity for, and oftener," he admitted. The result, he noted by July 2, was a point of diminishing return, requiring greater doses for relief. "Cocaine is a failure now," he told Douglas. "It hurts very much to apply it and I do not feel that it does me much good. I do not see why it should have afforded so much relief heretofore and now stopped."

As his time at Mt. McGregor continued and his work on the manuscript corrections progressed, Grant engaged in an awful tug of war. He tried to abstain as much as the excruciating pain would allow. "I feel the want of it very much. . . ." he admitted when he went without the drugs for even a day or two. "I think it better not to take it however because the injury done by it will be fed and kept up." The benefits were "but for a short time and . . . does only temporary good—very temporary."

Eventually, the agony in his throat became too much. "I do not see how I am to avoid the use of Cocain," he wrote to Douglas on July 10. "It would relieve me very much just now."

His misery came in many forms. Sleep often came restlessly. He had little appetite and frequent bouts of vomiting. The salts in the sedatives he took sweat themselves out across his forehead, leaving a gritty residue. "I feel that I am growing weaker all

Shrady and Douglas conferred frequently with each other and with Grant's family, although Grant himself had resigned himself to reading his newspapers on the cottage porch when he didn't have the energy to write. (loc)

the time," he told Fred. "Three of the sore places I immagine I can feel rotting out."

Grant told Douglas he could feel his system "preparing for dissolution" in three ways:

> *one by hemhorages, one by strangulation and the third by exhaustion. The first and second are liable to come at any moment to relieve me of my early sufferings; the time for the arrival of the third can be computed with almost mathematical certainty. With an increase of daily food I have [still] fallen off in weight and strength very rapidly for the last two weeks. There can not be a hope of going far beyond this time. All any physician, or any number of them do for me now is to make my burden of pain as light as possible.*

"I may last this month of July," he wrote to Fred, "but doubt it. Any hour may prove my last."

* * *

Despite the pain, Grant soldiered on with his work and put on a brave face for the rest of his family. "Do as I do. I take it quietly . . ." he wrote to them. "If I knew that the end was to be to-morrow I would try and get rest in the meantime."

"Do as I do," Grant advised his family. "I take it quietly . . ." (gc)

Grant also found relief from his work by entertaining visitors. Twain came at the end of June. "The old soldier battling with a deadly disease yet bravely completing his tasks, was a figure at once so pathetic and so noble. . ." he said.

A representative from the Catholic Church came on July 8 (Grant had feuded with the Church over the separation of church and state, so the appearance of the dignitary represented another act of reconciliation.) A delegation of Mexican journalists arrived later that day.

"I have been writing up my views of some of our generals, and of the character of Lincoln & Stanton," Grant wrote of his revisions. "I do not place Stanton as high as some people do. Mr. Lincoln cannot be extolled too highly." (cm)

On July 9, Charles Wood of Lansingburg, New York, made the trek up the mountain. Grant greeted him warmly, but apologized on a slip of paper, "I am very sorry that I am unable to converse even in a whisper." Grant expressed his deep gratitude to Wood for sending that first check those 15 months ago. "I feel very thankful to you for the kindness you did me last summer. I am glad to say that while there is much unblushing wickedness in this world yet there is a compensating generosity and grandeur of soul."

One of the most poignant accounts from the visitors of those Mt. McGregor days comes from Robert Underwood Johnson, editor of the *Century*, who paid his respects on July 9.

"The General, fully dressed, sat on the piazza in the sun, wearing something over his head, like a skullcap, and wrapped in a plaid shawl, looking thinner than before, and with a patient, resigned expression, but not with a stricken look," Johnson recalled. They had a warm meeting and Johnson assured Grant that the magazine bore no hard feelings about the book. They ended with a handshake. "I could hardly keep back the tears as I made my farewell to the great soldier who had saved the Union for all its people," Johnson wrote, "and to the man of warm and courageous heart who had fought his last battle for those he so tenderly loved."

The next visitor, one Grant appreciated "very highly," must have buoyed him tremendously. Simon Bolivar Buckner, a dear comrade from their days in the prewar army. In Mexico, after the war there had wrapped up, they had scaled the country's highest volcano together. When Grant left the service in disgrace in 1854, Buckner had loaned Grant the money to get back to Illinois.

Civil War had found them on opposite sides, and in 1862 at Ft. Donelson, Tennessee, they met on the battlefield. Grant won the confrontation and forced Buckner's acquiescence. "No terms except unconditional and immediate surrender can be accepted," Grant said—a phrase that made Grant a household name. Yet afterward, Grant took Buckner aside and made sure he had money in his pocket for the journey ahead as a POW.

Now at 62, Buckner was on his way back from his Niagara Falls honeymoon with his second wife, 28-year-old Delia Claiborne. Grant, delighted to see his old friend, had said he'd read all about the nuptials in the papers. "You look very natural," Grant told him, "except that your hair has whitened, and you have grown stouter."

A Kentuckian by birth, Simon Bolivar Buckner aged into the stereotypical visage of a Kentucky "colonel," although he had in fact risen to the rank of lieutenant general during the Civil War. He would also go on to serve a term as Kentucky's governor. (loc)

The two old friends traded reminiscences, and Grant delighted in Delia's company. In one of the longer passages of pencil-talk Grant wrote during those weeks, he revealed to Buckner that his illness, as awful as it had been, had good in it, too: "I have witnessed since my sickness just what I have wished to see ever since the war; harmony and good feeling between the sections. I have always contended that if there had been no body left but the soldiers we would have had peace in a year."

This echoed a sentiment Grant had articulated to Fred some days earlier: "The Confederate soldier vied with the Union soldier in sounding my praise. . . . It looks as if my sickness had had something to do to bring harmony between the sections. . . . Apparently I have accomplished more while apparently dying than it falls to the lot of most men to be able to do."

This, it turned out, would be the optimistic note he would end the *Memoirs* on: Pain and suffering—his own through cancer and the nation's through war—had redemptive powers. "I feel that we are on the eve of a new era, when there is to be great harmony between the Federal and Confederate," he concluded.

> *I cannot stay to be a living witness to the correctness of this prophecy; but I feel it within me that it is to be so. The universally kind feeling expressed for me at a time when it was supposed that each day would prove my last, seemed to me the beginning of the answer to "Let us have peace."*

Victory and Loss

Chapter Sixteen

Mid-July 1885

And so Grant passed those clear, warm days, sitting on the veranda. Julia often sat with him. When he worked, "[a] board was placed across the arms of the willow chair in which he sat, and, using this as a desk, the sick man wrote for a considerable time."

"I am sure I will never leave Mt. McGregor alive," he confided to his wife. "I pray God however that [I] may be spared to complete the necessary work upon my book."

Grant worked at it "almost continually," Dawson recounted of those days—at least as continually as Grant's fading strength allowed. "I saw that he was sinking fast and suffering intensely . . . " Dawson said.

Finally, by July 11, Grant felt like he had reached the home stretch. "I have my book off my mind now," he told Rev. Newman. "That relieves me of a tax upon my strength I could not avoid."

Still he kept editing, kept writing, kept revising. By July 17, he had added some 50 new pages. He told Douglas, "There is nothing more I should do to it now, and therefore I am not more likely to be more ready to go than at this moment."

And *still* he kept tweaking, kept changing, kept refining, kept improving. Every last detail had to be correct. "Should my career be closed at an earlier day," he instructed Julia, "I would be very glad if the boys would make arrangements to retain quarters here and go on with their work." He

The clock on the fireplace mantel in the cottage's main room still marks the time of Grant's death. (cm)

wanted to be sure the work would go on without him until done.

This was a legitimate concern, not only because of his own health but because of Fred's. The grueling pace and the emotional strain were taking their toll on him. "Fred," Grant wrote to him on July 22, "if you feel the least unwell, do not work until you feel like it. Your services are too important now to have you break down."

By then, Grant was done. The work, he knew, rested in the hands of others. "I saw at last that he had reached the end," Dawson said, "and all he could do was wait for death."

* * *

Two photographs of Grant emerge from these days. In both photos, he's seated in his wicker chair on the northeast corner of the cottage porch.

The more famous image, taken June 27, shows Grant tucked under a blanket with a pillow tucked behind his head. He wears a stocking cap. His legs are crossed and he has a tablet propped against one thigh as he writes. His eyes, cast down on the tablet, are angled downward so far that they nearly look

Grant on June 27, 1885 (loc)

closed. This has become the iconic image of Grant writing his memoirs—huddled up, hard at work, focused only on finishing.

In the second image—the last photograph taken of him alive—comes from July 20, the day he finished his *Memoirs*. His eyes are again downcast, this time at a newspaper, but he appears ready to lift his gaze over the top rims of his round spectacles at the photographer. His legs are still crossed, although he's shed his blanket, revealing slippers. His suit looks looser than it did even three weeks earlier. Most striking is the top hat, which makes him look proper, ready to go out or ready to receive company, in spite of the slippers.

Grant on July 20, 1885 (loc)

This is not the writer at work but at rest.

We can see how he looked on the day he—quite literally—finished his life's work.

* * *

"One day he put aside his pencil and said there was nothing more to do."

That's how Mark Twain described it: Monday, July 20, 1885.

Eleven months . . . two volumes . . . 1,231 pages . . . 291,000 words.

Grant is sitting in his face-to-face chairs in his room when he finishes. He sets down his pencil with an audible click on the table next to him: the sound of finality.

No account exists of that moment, but it's a moment all writers relish, the moment they finally realize it's okay to let a piece of writing *go*. It's relief and a soaring internal exultation, and the exhaustion nipping at the periphery is nothing more than a familiar work companion.

It's reasonable to imagine Dawson there in the room with him, and Fred, and probably Terrell, and maybe McSweeney, who is at least in the adjacent

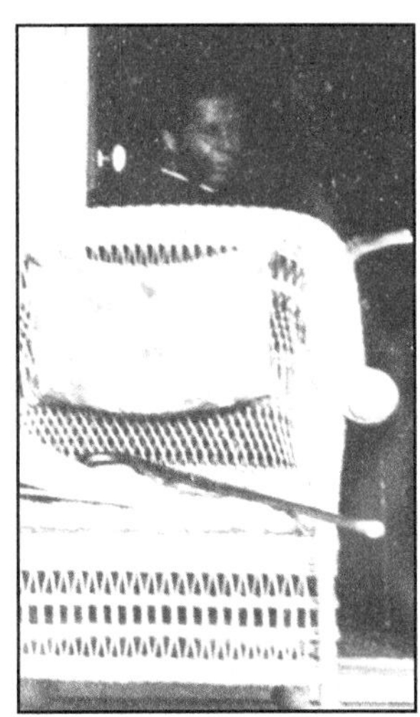

Harrison Terrell appears in one of the last photos taken of Grant. Terrell kept nearby at all times, always able to anticipate Grant's needs. Among a supporting cast that includes Twain, Sherman, Vanderbilt, Barnum, and others, he remains one of the great unsung heroes of Grant's story. (loc)

"What do you think of my taking the bath wagon and going down to overlook the south view?" Grant scribbled. Sam Willett pulled while Harrison Terrell pushed. (gc)

anteroom. It's reasonable to imagine Fred calling to Julia. *Mother, he's done,* he says, pleased. Julia comes into the room, makes eye contact with her Ulys, and although he cannot speak, that's enough. He smiles and nods. She lights up.

To celebrate, Grant suggests a trip down to a scenic overlook some 150 yards away from the cottage. Terrell, Fred, Douglas, and others wheel into motion.

In the bustle, Grant slips into his coat pocket the letter he'd written to Julia shortly after arriving at the cottage. He also slips in the ring she'd given him and the locks of her hair and Buck's.

He's ready. In all the ways he needs to be, he's ready.

He has finished his life's work. There will be no turning back.

* * *

A modern path invites visitors to take in the overview's charms for themselves. (cm)

The overlook offers an open vista of the Hudson Valley and makes Mt. McGregor such a spectacular place to visit. Such an expansive view would certainly have reflected Grant's feelings in those moments of post-writing triumph.

But the short trip down to the overlook

"There is a spot here known as the Eastern Outlook, which few visitors fail to see and which is a delight to all," the *New York Times* reported on July 21, 1885. "It commands a broad sweep of the valley, with the Green Mountains banking the eastern horizon, the Adirondacks looming up in the north, and the Catskills traced against the southern sky. One may rest there in rustic chairs under a pavilion ingeniously built of tree limbs and branches yet in the bark, and look out upon a scene that has no equal for pastoral repose in this region."(gc)

exhausted Grant, who rode in the Bath chair. After a brief rest, the party sought a shortcut back to the cottage. But as the old saying goes, "Shortcuts make long delays," and the trip back went awry. The new path through the woods led to a spur of the rail line, littered with heaps of coal and other detritus, all of which Grant had to navigate by foot and by cane.

Back at the cottage, Grant collapsed back into his double chairs. He slept all night and on and off throughout the next day. By evening, his family noticed that he didn't appear to be coming out of his daze.

Douglas secured a bed from the hotel and had it installed in the large front room of the cottage. It was cooler there than in Grant's room, and Douglas felt the better air circulation would help his patient. For the first time in months, Grant was moved from his chair into an actual bed. As it happened, a portrait of Lincoln hung on the wall above the spot where the bed best fit. A few feet to the left of the portrait was one of Grant himself.

An examination revealed a higher temperature and an erratic pulse. Douglas summoned Dr. Shrady, on call at his home in Hudson. He also called in Buck and his family. Reporters were alerted.

When Buck arrived the next day, July 22, Grant recognized him and tried to speak, but his voice failed him. Only later, with the family and his retinue of doctors crowded around him, did Grant finally muster words: "I don't want anybody to feel distressed on my account."

The hours of the evening unspooled slow and long. "As the hours grew on, the symptoms

Today, a monument marks the spot where the pavilion once stood. From here, it says, Grant took in his last view of the panorama. (cm)

"THE LORD WILL STRENGTHEN HIM UPON THE BED OF LANGUISHING; THOU WILT MAKE ALL HIS BED IN HIS SICKNESS."
— A poem, "The Everlasting Arms," that now hangs in Grant's death room at the cottage, quoting one of the Psalms

The bed (above, right) furnished by the hotel for Grant was cleverly designed so that it folded up to look like a desk. As a desk, though (above), it was not functional. (cm)(gc)

of dissolution grew," Douglas observed. "The respiration quickened, the pulse became small and very frequent, the respiration shallower and quicker, the pulse too frequent to be counted. . . ."

Are you in pain? Fred asked his father.

"No," Grant replied aloud.

Can we get you anything?

"Water."

The one thing that had felt like molten lead going down his throat was now the only thing that offered relief. The nurse, McSweeny, wet Grant's mouth with a damp towel.

Julia sat next to Grant's bedside. When she spoke, he would open his eyes and gaze at her.

On the fireplace mantel, a small porcelain clock ticked away the minutes.

* * *

The quiet hours of dawn soon erupted into a flurry of activity. Family members who had retired upstairs overnight at Douglas's urging bolted downstairs. The other doctors hurried down from the hotel. All gathered in the large room, around the bed beneath Lincoln's portrait.

A noticeable change had come over Grant's features, and his breathing had become soft and quick. His bare throat, so long the cradle of his agony, quivered with each quickened breath.

Not visible in this sketch of Grant's death room is the portrait of Grant that hung on the wall to the left of Lincoln's. (gc)

"The outer air, gently moving, swayed the curtains at an east window," *The New York Times* recounted. "Into the crevice crept a white ray from the sun. It reached across the room like a rod and lighted [the] picture of Lincoln over the deathbed. The sun did not touch the companion picture, which was of the General."

Julia held her husband's hand. Fred stroked his father's brow.

Moments passed in silence.

"The light on the portrait of Lincoln was still sinking," the *Times* continued;

> *presently the General opened his eyes and glanced about him, looking into the faces of all. The glance lingered as it met the tender gaze of his companion. A startled, wavering motion at the throat, a few quiet gasps, a sigh, and the appearance of falling into a gentle sleep followed. . . . He lay without motion. At that instant the window curtain swayed back in place, shutting out the sunbeam.*

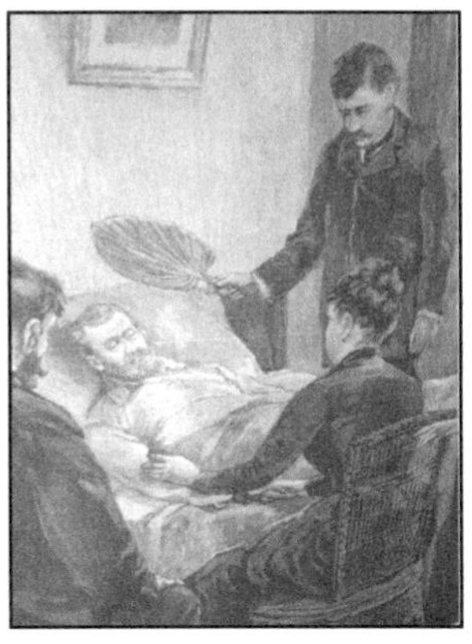

In Grant's final moments, his family gathered 'round. (fl)

Julia silently buried her face in her handkerchief. Fred, kneeling by his father's bedside, rose and crossed the room to the clock on the fireplace mantel. As Douglas confirmed Grant's death, Fred stopped the clock's hands.

8:08 a.m. Thursday, July 23, 1885.

Ulysses S. Grant had beaten death by three days.

Chapter Seventeen

July 24, 1885—Present

"[I]f he should die there, it might make the place a national shrine," one of the owners of the Balmoral Hotel said as Grant first considered his move to Mt. McGregor.

In a sense, that prediction has become true, although Grant Cottage is actually a *state* historic site—overseen by New York's Office of Parks, Recreation, and Historic Preservation and operated by a vibrant "friends group," Friends of Grant Cottage. It remains a national shrine—and an international shrine, for that matter—because it continues to attract visitors from all around the world.

The cottage looks much as it did in 1885. Pine yellow with maroon and evergreen trim, it stands sentinel like on the slope of the hill, peeking out from the glade of oaks and maples that shade it. It feels like a shy animal on the edge of a treeline, watching visitors as they approach.

Inside, in Grant's room, the tall glass apothecary tube, still partially filled with cocaine water, catches late-afternoon light from a northwest window. Grant's twin leather chairs still stare at each other. A glass-door cabinet displays Grant's nightshirt, his hair brush and moustache brush, a blood-pressure cuff, and his beaver top hat.

In the front room, the bed Grant died in remains in the same spot it was in on the morning Grant died, the portraits of Lincoln and Grant still

"Let us have peace." (cm)

Top: Grant's bed was removed and a temporary bier was constructed in the room forr viewing. Bottom: Funeral arrangements sent in 1885 were hand-dipped in wax to preserve them and remain on display. Heaven's Gate (right) came from Leland Stanford, founder of Stanford University. The gate is ajar to represent the open gates awaiting Grant. The pillow (center) with the sword and four stars came from the George Gordon Meade post of the GAR. Grant was the first four-star general in American history. The cross and sword (left) came from Mrs. Amos Bissel, a Coloradoan who advocated equal suffrage. Below: Fred slipped his father's engagement ring back onto Grant's finger; Grant had taken it off because his weight-loss had made it too loose. (gc)(cm)(fl)

holding vigil. In a nearby corner, Grant's favorite wicker chair, empty, waits for the general's return. A reproduction sits on the opposite side of the door, out on the porch, where visitors can sit in the same spot Grant favored. I have sat there myself and thought of the general.

In the death room, the porcelain clock on the fireplace mantle still waits at 8:08 for orders to resume its march—orders that will never come.

Grant remained at the cottage after his death until August 4—a total of two weeks. During that time, his body was embalmed while final preparations were made for his funeral and burial in New York City. Meanwhile, condolences came in from around the country and around the world. Several large floral displays—since preserved in wax and still on display in the cottage's dining room—helped mask the odor of slow summer decomposition.

TOP: On the day Grant's body was finally removed from Mt. McGregor, visitors filed through the main room to pay their respects. BOTTOM: Rev. Newman officiated at a sermon on the cottage porch. "The keenest, closest, broadest of all observers, he was the most silent of men," Newman declared. BELOW: Grant's funeral train. (gc)(gc)(gc)

On August 3, a small private service was held at the cottage. At 2 o'clock, a storm set in. "It was not a hard rain but a searching and persistent one," a newspaper reported. "Vapor began to fill the valley like a milky sea, and the air grew uncomfortable. . . ." Otherwise, said the paper, "[t]he last full day of the stay of Gen. Grant's body at this place will be remembered as one of sadness and quiet.

Julia would stay at the cottage for a month longer, accompanied by Rev. Newman's wife, while her husband's body was taken down from the mountain—first to Saratoga, then on to Albany, where a larger service was held on August 5.

The largest of the funeral services, the one in New York City, was scheduled for Saturday, August

Winfield Scott Hancock, a West Point classmate of Grant's, had been Grant's favored commander during the 1864 Overland Campaign. Hancock's II Corps was repeatedly given the most difficult assignments because of Hancock's dependability and reputation for hard fighting. Sadly, Grant sang an entirely different tune during the 1880 presidential campaign, when Hancock was the Democratic candidate and Grant, favoring fellow Republican James Garfield, campaigned against him. "I have known [Hancock] for forty years," Grant said. "He is a vain, weak man. He is the most selfish man I know." (loc)

Scenes from Grant's funerals: in Albany (top); his coffin in New York City (middle); veterans of the Grand Army of the Republic and a multitude of spectators—including, somewhere in the mass, Ferdinand Ward (bottom). (loc)(loc)(loc)

8. "The day broke heavy and sullen, as though the smoke of his hundred battles yet hung in the sky," recorded *The New York Times*.

President Grover Cleveland placed one of Grant's former subordinates, Maj. Gen. Winfield Scott Hancock, in charge of the proceedings. Among the honorary pallbearers: Simon Bolivar Buckner and another former Confederate general, Joseph E. Johnston. Grant's friends Joseph Drexel and George Childs served, too.

"North and South reunited again," a newspaper artist wrote, suggesting the shared grief of the nation as reflected among the pallbearers, who included Sherman, Johnston, and Buckner. (loc)

With 60,000 participants and several thousand horse-and-carriage teams, the funeral procession through Manhattan ran six miles long, with stops along the way to refresh many of the aging veterans who would take part. "[A]s far as the eye could measure the avenue," said *The New York Times*, "were massed the regiments in their brilliant uniforms, their guns glistening in the sun, their colors draped, and their slow steps keeping time to the music of many dirges for the dead."

A million spectators turned out to mourn, making it a funeral pageant larger even than Abraham Lincoln's. One of those spectators, Ferdinand Ward, bribed his way out of jail so he could watch the procession.

"[E]very balcony, window, and door commanding a view of the line of march was teeming," the Times reported;

> *the roofs and cornices swarmed; there was not an accessible point, however high and dangerous, but had its observer; men climbed the telegraph poles and clung to the wires; boys were high in the trees; carriages thronged the crossings; . . .the statues in the squares were black with climbers, and even the lamp posts granted many a foothold."*

As Grant's final resting place, Julia had selected Riverside Park, a beautiful spot high atop the bluffs overlooking the Hudson. Grant's casket was

Top: Tens of thousands of people crammed Riverside Park. "[E]very face was sad," said Grant's granddaughter, "and some of them were weeping." Bottom: A temporary tomb would house Grant's body for twelve years while a more suitable rest place was constructed. Opposite: A cartoon in Puck paid tribute to Grant. (gc)(loc)

placed inside a hastily constructed temporary tomb, although plans for a larger, grander permanent tomb were already underway (see Appendix).

On the river, warships fired their cannons in salute. On the bluff, dignitaries offered two hours' worth of speeches. "The various regiments and bands, moving here and halting there, formed a kaleidoscope of the most brilliant covers," the *Times* said.

Mourners wept. William T. Sherman, presenting the flag from Grant's coffin to Fred, sobbed openly.

"The march of another comrade is over. . ." said a chaplain in the GAR.

"Through the stillness the low, sweet notes of the soldier's good-night," the *Times* intoned. "Put out the lights—the great doors were closed and no eye beheld him but that of his God."

* * *

PEACE, AND THE GOOD WILL OF ALL MEN.

Another Lesson for the "Bloody Shirt" Patriots.

Grant's Tomb was finished in 1897 and is now operated by the National Park Service. (cm)

Grant's Tomb would go through its own rise and fall and rise in fortunes (see Appendix A), but Grant Cottage would plug along in steady fashion thanks to the stalwart attention of generations of friends and caretakers. "[I]n the years following his death," writes historian Steven Trimm, a guide at Grant Cottage who often portrays Grant in living history programs, "dedicated individuals collected, preserved and passed along stories about the hero of the Civil War, the 18th president, Ulysses S. Grant and the closing days of his life on Mount McGregor."

Grant Cottage caretaker Oliver P. Clarke wrote one of the earliest histories of Grant's final days. (gc)

Recognizing the site's importance, Joseph Drexel never occupied his mountaintop cottage; instead, he offered the building to the national government for preservation. The government declined, so Drexel turned to the Grand Army of the Republic. In conjunction with the state of New York and a newly formed Mount McGregor Memorial Association, The GAR provided leadership and funding to keep

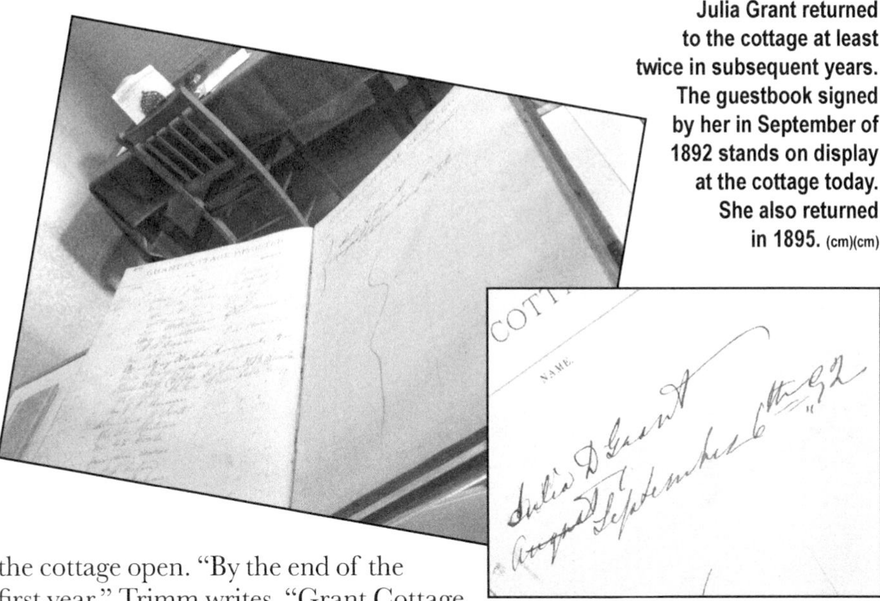

Julia Grant returned to the cottage at least twice in subsequent years. The guestbook signed by her in September of 1892 stands on display at the cottage today. She also returned in 1895. (cm)(cm)

the cottage open. "By the end of the first year," Trimm writes, "Grant Cottage had drawn 15,000 visitors."

The list of caretakers reads like a who's-who of American demographics: Oliver P. Clarke, a Union veteran and Andersonville Prison survivor; Josie Clarke, Oliver's widow, who'd been a housewife all her life; Suye Narita, an immigrant from Japan who became the Clarke's surrogate "daughter"; and, finally, the Friends of Grant Cottage.

The Balmoral Hotel burned in the winter of 1897. "The blaze was so spectacular," Trimm recounts, "firefighters ten miles away in Saratoga thought at first the town was aflame. That the inferno spared Grant Cottage was a miracle."

In 1949, caretaker Suye Narita hosted Ulysses S. Grant III, the grandson of the late president, who had last been at the cottage as a four-year-old during the fateful summer of 1885. (gc)

In the years that followed, a tuberculosis sanitarium sprung up on the mountaintop. It was for treatment at that sanitarium that Suye, then a 13-year-old girl, came to Mt. McGregor in 1914. She stayed until her death in 1984. A monument in her honor stands today in front of the cottage.

The sanitarium, meanwhile, eventually became a rest camp for veterans, then a school for the developmentally disabled, then a medium-security

While the Balmoral Hotel is nothing but a whisper in the hilltop wind, Mt. McGregor has since hosted (bottom) a tuberculosis sanitarium, a mental health ward, and (top) a medium-security prison. Grant Cottage has had to tap into those state facilities for water, sewer, and electricity, so when New York closed the prison in 2014, it temporarily cast doubt on the viability of keeping the cottage open. Shortly thereafter, the site was assigned as a unit of Moreau State Park to insure its continued operation. (cm)(cm)

RIGHT: A bronze tablet in front of Grant Cottage, erected in 1916 by the New York division of the Sons of Union Veterans to memorialize the events that took place there, also bears a small memorial plaque on its face, "In memory of Suye Gambino Caring for Grant Cottage 1914-1984." (cm)

ABOVE AND RIGHT: Suye Narita Gambino died in 1984 and wished to be buried within site of Grant Cottage. "Because the prison occupied so much of the mountain top, this wasn't possible," explains Grant Cottage historian Steve Trimm. Suye and her husband, Tony, are instead buried near the front of Gurn Spring Cemetery, near the I-87 interchange, within site of Mt. McGregor. The Eastern Overlook, "where," says Trimm, "for so many years, Suye reverently raised and lowered her American flag," is visible in the distance. (cm)(cm)

state prison. In 2014, the prison closed, leaving Grant Cottage alone atop the mountain.

"It's a special place," Trimm tells me on a visit in May 2015. On this day some 130 years earlier, Grant was pushing through his book, fuming over Badeau's betrayal, having the very earliest conversations about possibly leaving Manhattan for the summer. Some 21 years before that, in 1864, he was grappling with Lee's forces on the muddy battlefield around Spotsylvania Court House.

Those struggles, Trimm says, in many ways typify the sorts of struggles that illustrate Grant's

ABOVE LEFT: Steve Trimm, a retired mental health professional, brings Grant's story to life at Grant Cottage through living history. He most frequently portrays Grant during his last weeks at Mt. McGregor, but at other times he portrays programs as Fred Grant; GAR member Sam Willett; original cottage caretaker Oliver Clarke; and landowner Duncan McGregor. "I have come to believe that the best way to teach history is by telling a good story," says Trimm, who has a background in community theater. "One of the best ways to do that is to present it as if it's your own, as if you've lived it." ABOVE RIGHT: The Friends of Grant Cottage offer daily tours of the building during the summer and fall, and they also host a variety of special events and speakers, such as this bedside program in Grant's death room on the anniversary of his death. "Working here is a team effort," Trimm says. The stewardship of the Friends, who operate the state-owned site through an agreement with New York State, serves as a model public-citizen partnership. (gc)(gc)

In 2005, the Friends of Grant Cottage opened a visitor center on the grounds. The building, a former arts-and-crafts-style stone garage built in 1913, is leased from the state of New York, which owns the property. Renovations, which began in 2003, cost $125,000—a combination of state money and private funds raised by the Friends. The center features a number of displays about Grant's life, career, and last days; meeting space; and a bookstore. (cm)

humanity—and, in turn, make Grant a role model for him. "These struggles we all have to be moral/ethical/good people—our forbearers all went through that," Trimm explains. "The details differ, but the essence of the struggle remains the same."

Trimm speaks in the same straightforward, clear style that Grant wrote with, so he pauses to collect his next thought. "Lincoln said we should listen to the better angels of our nature," he finally says. "Grant always did—and he stands as proof that we can, too."

* * *

On the cottage porch, a wooden Adirondack chair now sits in the spot where Grant so often sat. His original chair sits just inside the door, facing his deathbed.

"All that was inspiring about Grant—the way he faced death; the way, even in his last hours, that he cared for his family—maybe it all comes together for us here," Trimm tells me. "All of us talk about how being on that porch feels for us. It touches us all in very positive ways."

I settle into the chair on the porch and sit there for a few moments. The birds sing and the breeze rustles the leaves ever so slightly. I try to channel a little of Grant's spirit and can feel him there in these stories. I can hear the shuffle of his feet across the floorboards and the hollow thump of his cane on the wood.

I can hear the rustle of turning pages as he writes, writes, writes. . . .

A sketch of the western overlook as it appeared in July 1885 (gc)

PERSONAL MEMOIRS OF U. S. GRANT

The Last Word

EPILOGUE

William Dean Howells, the era's great arbiter of literature, had lunched with Twain and Grant the day Twain first suggested that Grant write his memoirs. That had been in 1881. Five years later, he finally had the chance to see the final fruits of that conversation.

"I am reading Grant's book with the delight I find to fail in novels," he wrote to his good friend Twain. "The book merits its enormous success, simply as literature." He judged the piece "a masterpiece."

Twain issued the memoirs in five different bindings that ranged in price from a basic $7 set to $25 leather-bound edition. Twain's subscription salesmen ultimately sold more than 300,000 sets. The books began appearing on December 10, 1885, and by February, Twain presented Julia a royalty check for $200,000. It would go on to earn more than $450,000 in royalties in its first two years.

An a publicly published assessment of Grant's book, Howells wrote:

> *[T]hese Personal Memoirs of U. S. Grant, written as simply and straight forwardly as his battles were fought, couched in the most unpretentious phrase, with never a touch of grandiosity or attitudinizing, familiar, homely, even common in style, is a great piece of literature, because great literature is nothing more nor less than the clear expression of minds that have something great in them. . . .*

Grant's Memoirs have never gone out of print. This first edition is on display at the Grant's Tomb visitor center in New York City. (cm)

William Dean Howells, an author and highly influential editor of *The Atlantic Monthly*, advocated a literary movement called "Realism," which emphasized a faithful representation of reality and a truth in detail called "verisimilitude." It's little wonder he admired Grant's straightforward, factual style of writing. (loc)

Julia wrote memoirs of her own, *The Personal Memoirs of Julia Dent Grant (Mrs. Ulysses S. Grant)*. However, they weren't published until nearly 80 years later, in 1975. According to the National Park Service, Julia's memoirs "were considered too close to the private life of her husband to be published in the 1890s." (loc)

Perhaps most telling of the *Memoirs*' value: In the 130 years since they were published, Grant's memoirs have never gone out of print.

"Other books of the war will be forgotten, mislaid, dismissed. Millions will read Grant's Memoirs and remember them," predicted Grant's close friend, William T. Sherman, himself the author of an excellent Civil War memoir.

Another friend, editorial cartoonist Thomas Nast, admitted "it was initially hard for me to read his book, but his words bring forth his sprit, his humanity, his goodness. He wrote as he talked, simple, unadorned, manly. He was the most complete and masculine person I ever knew, and his book is the most complete book I have ever read."

Not all reaction was positive. In the north, many of Grant's political rivals dismissed the book; across the South, unreconstructed former Confederates were similarly dismissive. *The Southern Historical Society Papers* reviewed the memoirs as "a book full of blunders and flat contradictions of the official reports (both Federal and Confederate), and the future historian who attempts to follow it will be led very far from the truth."

Modern scholar Joan Waugh has assessed the *Memoirs* as "a deliberately triumphal narrative of the Civil War written from the viewpoint of the man most closely identified with bring about Northern victory."

"Looking back didn't come to Grant naturally," surmises Grant Cottage's Steve Trimm. "His

The green-cloth "shoulder strap" edition evoked Grant's general's stars and cost $7/set. A light brown full-sheepskin binding with marbled edges cost $9/set. A dark brown set with half morocco binding and marbled edges cost $11/set. The other two versions were leather bound with gilt edges that sold for $18 and $25/set. (cm)

sudden poverty and terminal diagnosis forced this on him. But he became enthusiastic about it. It was important to him to state his view of things."

The South had lost militarily and Lost Cause propagandists, through their own postwar writings, were desperate to convince posterity that they'd at least won a moral victory, Trimm explains. "Northerners who wanted to forget the war colluded with them, in a way, because they just got worn out and fed up with re-litigating the deepest causes and meanings of the war. The Northerners finally said, in effect, 'We won, and that's all that counts. We will never agree on the war's meaning. But the one point we can concede is that the Confederate soldiers were valiant. We will agree that they were as valiant and sincere as the Yankee soldiers.' That was their concession."

However, Grant saw his memoirs as a chance to unequivocally state that the war was all about treason. "Grant was not willing to forget that," says Trimm. "The South's was not a noble cause; the war was not a mere misunderstanding. It was a fight to the death, and it involved treason."

Nicknamed "Lee's Bad Old Man," the irascible Jubal Early (left) remained an unrepentant, un-Reconstructed Rebel until the day he died. The prickly Daniel Harvey Hill (right) had difficulty getting along with anyone during the war, but his work editing the Southern Historical Society's Papers helped him channel his ire. Both ex-generals served as powerful anti-North voices and shaped what became known as the Lost Cause mythology. Both men hated Grant and blamed him for the South's loss in the Civil War, so they spent considerable time trying to tear down his reputation. (loc)(loc)

With that as context, a comment Grant made during his Mt. McGregor conversation with Simon Buckner now stands out as deeply ironic: "Jubel [Jubal] Early and [D. H.] Hill are the only two that I know of who do not seem to be satisfied on the southern side," Grant told his old friend, practically dismissing the embittered, un-Reconstructed Rebels. He had, in the previous few years, expressed some concern about the rising "Lost Cause" interpretation of the war, with Early and Hill as its leading apostles. Grant saw his memoirs as an important countermeasure to that mythology.

So did Early and Hill. The Lost Cause could not survive if Grant's interpretation of the truth gained wide acceptance. It—and Grant himself—had to be discredited if the South were ever to win the peace. As a result, disgruntled Lost Causers took steady, unrelenting aim at Grant, particularly after his death. Grant's reputation has suffered ever since as a result. "It is one thing to fight it out if it takes all summer," says historian Brooks D. Simpson; "it is quite another to continue to fight along that line for another century and a half."

Grant conversed with Buckner with the optimistic assurance of a man who felt he had successfully secured his own legacy and the meaning of the war. He had no way to know just how ascendant the Lost Cause interpretation was at the time, or how powerfully it would stick in the public imagination during the century and a half that followed.

After winning the war and writing its story, Grant would have been puzzled to wonder how he could have possibly lost the peace.

***The Personal Memoirs of Ulysses S. Grant*, which sprung from Grant's work on articles for Century Magazine, has become one of the most influential resources for Civil War researchers.** (cm)

Grant's Tomb

APPENDIX A
by Pat Tintle

It was a mid-March morning as I made my way through the hilly streets of upper Manhattan. Having just walked up the stairs from the #1 train, my first site as I stepped onto West 116th Street was the historic campus of Columbia University. But I had my eyes set on another landmark—the tomb of President Ulysses S. Grant.

Tracking back to 1888, the Grant Monument Association, led by the first black graduate of Harvard University, Richard Greener, proposed an architectural competition for the design of the president's tomb. The competition came three years after Grant's death due to a long process of collecting funds. Disappointed by the submissions, the Grant Monument Association held a second competition limited to five prominent architectural firms, ultimately awarding the job to John Hemenway Duncan, the architect of numerous New York City landmarks including the Soldiers' and Sailors' Memorial Arch in Brooklyn and the Hotel Wolcott in midtown Manhattan.

There had been national debate over the location of the Grant monument. Many Americans believed that a proper resting place should be installed somewhere in Washington, D.C., but First Lady Julia Dent Grant wished the tomb to be positioned in New York City, citing the city as the president's desired resting location and the fact that the sheer population of New York would bring in more visitors than anywhere else in the country.

The dedication of Grant's Tomb on April 27, 1897—the 75th anniversary of Grant's birth—drew nearly as many spectators as his funeral twelve years earlier. President McKinley and Julia Grant presided over festivities. Julia was laid to rest there after she passed away in 1902. (cm)

Duncan's work, completed in 1897 in the Morningside Heights section of Riverside Park, is the very design that stands today. The granite and marble tomb features a 70-foot dome topped with a sharp, prominent conical roof. The exterior also includes six classical columns, creating an extraordinary stage as visitors enter the structure after climbing the granite staircase.

The high-domed ceiling of Grant's Tomb rises seventy feet above the main level, creating a grand, majestic air. (cm)

As I walked toward the presidential resting place, it was obvious how grand the structure must have been for its time, considering many of the surrounding buildings were not in place back in 1897. That made the tomb a landmark in 19th century New York.

Atop the tomb's staircase, I greet Columbia University graduate Frank Scaturro for a tour of the tomb. A New York attorney, Scaturro has a strong knowledge of and fascination for a president whom he describes as "the only true civil rights president we had between emancipation and the mid-20th century." Scaturro is also the man who helped save Grant's Tomb.

By 1997, Grant's Tomb had no longer become a suitable resting place for a former United States commander in chief. The structure actually resembled more of the West 116th subway station I exited rather than a tomb for an American icon. Graffiti covered the walls that, 100 years prior, Duncan had designed.

Not only were the walls poisoned with

Who's sleeping in Grant's tomb? For years, homeless people, such as the person stretched out against the far wall (left), sought shelter there. Meanwhile, vandals desecrated the tomb with graffiti and littered its steps with used condoms and dime bags (below). (fs)(fs)

territorial markings, but a consistent odor of urine and feces lurked around the tomb, including the portico area that served as the Tomb's entrance. Drug paraphernalia scattered around the structure only proved the tomb to be more of a homeless haven than a memorial described by Duncan as "a monumental structure that should be unmistakably a tomb of military character." Instead of resting with honor, Grant rested among drug users and criminals.

"The homeless would camp out right up the stairs, and when I walked into the tomb, I'd have to hold my breath because there was a urine stench," Scaturro recalls. "There was evidence that they were not only using the site as a bathroom, but also we would find dime bags and crack vials because they would do drugs on a pretty rampant basis."

Scaturro saw another issue with the tomb, too. At the time of its completion, Grant's Tomb was not tucked away, hidden among skyscrapers and apartment complexes. This was pre-Empire State Building New York, so, being placed on one of the highest points of the island, Grant's Tomb was visible from as far away as lower Manhattan. It had an iconic aura similar to that of the Statue of Liberty.

"Who's buried in Grant's Tomb?" was a recurring question on Groucho Marx's game show *You Bet Your Life*. He would offer it as a softball to contestants who needed an easy question. Technically, the answer is "No one" because Grant is entombed in an above-ground mausoleum, not buried in an underground grave, but Marx generously accepted "Grant" as an answer. (w)

But times changed.

While die-hard New York history buffs may know the meaning of the neoclassical-designed tomb, it would be difficult for the common New York resident to recite any historical background of the structure. Gone are the days when Groucho Marx could propose his question of "Who's buried in Grant's Tomb?" to the average Manhattanite.

Even the area immediately surrounding Grant's Tomb provides no indication of its historical significance. A tall line of trees—which were not part of the land's original design, blocks much of the tomb's view as a New Yorker walks up Riverside Drive. And a contemporary "art project," *The Rolling Bench,* plagues the atmosphere with distracting colors and irrelevant images more suitable for a children's playground than a marker of American history.

Despite being an eyesore, *The Rolling Bench* had initial intentions of improving the community surrounding the tomb. Designed by Pedro Silva and sponsored by the non-profit organization CityArts, the project was completed in 1972 and, at the time, was reportedly the largest public art project in U.S. history. Silva stated the purpose of the mosaic-covered benches was "to celebrate the 100th anniversary of Yellowstone as the first national

Above: On its own, The Rolling Bench looks funky and fun, but it contrasts gaudily against the classical architecture of the tomb. Right: By 1980, despite its attempt at community reclamation, even the bench had fallen on hard times. (cm)(fs)

Ulysses and Julia Grant rest side by side in the tomb's lower level. An open circular gallery allows visitors to gaze down on the red granite sarcofigi, although a stairway provides access to the ground floor. Each sarcophagus weighs eight and a half tons. (cm)

Three mosaic murals by Allyn Cox were installed in three overhead lunettes and dedicated in 1966. Grant's handshake with Lee at Appomattox reflects off the surface of the Grants' coffins. (cm)

park in the world, signed by Grant when he was president" and to "make this place more frequented by people." The benches also saw a restoration of their own in 2008, as Silva supervised local volunteers and children who reworked the benches by hand.

But Silva's mission has only hurt the area, says Scaturro.

"The most regrettable Park Service decision was the installation of these mosaic benches," Scaturro laments. "They thought, 'Let's make this place more relevant to the surrounding community; never mind the guy buried there who bears colossal importance to our history.' So they put in these benches, and never has the tomb faced worse days than after these things were installed."

Starting in 1991, while he was an undergraduate at Columbia, Scaturro led the movement to restore

Grant's Tomb. At first, the National Park Service largely ignored his efforts, but Scaturro managed to get the attention of Congress with his 300-page report, issued in 1993, citing the treatment of the tomb as a national disgrace. Scaturro's report was also sent to President Bill Clinton and later received notable media coverage.

"Murals have been painted out and replaced with photographs that are now frayed," *The New York Times* reported in an opinion piece on Jan. 2, 1994. "A display of photocopied pictures and a sampling of Grant's words shows that someone cared, but lacked funds for a more professional mounting." Scaturro's effort also prompted *The Times* to endorse his funding proposal: "[T]he tomb's lamentable condition demands more funds from Washington, at least enough to clean up, patch up and restore honor to the heroic commander who became the nation's 18th President."

Antechambers house flags from various units Grant was associated with, and the walls are painted with battle map-like murals that depict his many battles. (cm)(cm)

Scaturro went so far as to sue both the National Park Service, which took over management of the site in 1959, and the Interior Department for their neglect of the tomb's condition.

"[The National Park Service] really didn't know what to do with the site," Scaturro says. "They were designed originally to administer sites like Yellowstone and Yosemite, but they really didn't know what to do with these historical treasures."

Scaturro's efforts were ultimately successful; the site's budget was tripled, and $1.8 million was appropriated for restoration, which was completed in 1997, the 100th anniversary of the tomb's dedication.

The difference between the 1980s version of Grant's Tomb and the 2015 version is noticeable the moment one steps onto the granite stairs. Today, the tomb is properly maintained by park rangers, who are all more than willing to discuss the presidency of Grant, as well as the history of the tomb itself. The two granite sarcophagi, which hold both Grant and the First Lady, are on proud display under the beautifully, naturally lit dome designed by Duncan. Busts of Civil War generals surround the bodies of the Grants—as if guarding the president and first lady—adding historical context to an honorable resting place for the United States' 18th president.

While Grant's Tomb may never be as world-famous as it was in the early 20th century, Scaturro's efforts have undoubtedly saved the site from irrelevance. Those who are interested in one of the country's most notable and debated military and political leaders can fully take in the significance of Grant's legacy without having to step over trash or feeling endangered in Duncan's structure.

Grant's Tomb is a New York and national landmark. It is a unique and important mausoleum positioned along the scenic banks of the Hudson River and just across the street from Riverside Church. Dozens of college students and locals pass the tomb everyday, but perhaps too few are familiar with the story that has become a part of their daily commute. But, as Scaturro's restoration efforts continue, the tomb may see a renaissance of awareness in years to come.

Busts of Grant's top lieutenants hold vigil in alcoves that overlook the Grants' sarcophagi: Phil Sheridan, Ord, George Thomas, James McPherson, and Sherman (above), who still looks especially haunted by the loss of his friend. Unfortunately missing is George Gordon Meade, slighted because he was not one of Grant's cronies from the Western Theater. (cm)

PAT TINTLE *is a correspondent for Emerging Civil War <www.emergingcivilwar.com>.*

Memorializing Grant

APPENDIX B

by Kathleen Logothetis Thompson and Chris Mackowski

(w)

Kings Canyon National Park, California (1867)
The General Grant tree is a giant sequoia in California's Kings Canyon National Park, said to be the second-largest tree in the world. Standing more than 267 feet tall and more than 107 feet around, it's thought to be around 1,600 years old. President Coolidge dubbed in the nation's Christmas tree in 1926, and in 1956, President Eisenhower declared it a national memorial to all those who've died in war.

Ueno Park, Tokyo (1879)
During his world tour, Grant spent an extended period in Japan and, as part of a civic ceremony in Tokyo, planted trees in the park. Fifty years later, a plaque featuring a relief of Grant was installed to commemorate the ceremony (below, left). He also planted a cedar tree near the Zojoji temple, which is also marked with a plaque (below, right).

(w)

(rb)

(bp)

City Hall, St. Louis (1888)
The St. Louis statue by local sculptor Robert Porter Bringhurst is one of the earliest of Grant. The nine-and-a-half-foot statue stands on a 10-foot granite pedestal on the north side of city hall. Grant is portrayed as a stout figure in military uniform, field glasses in hand and sword on hip.

(bs)

Fort Leavenworth, Kansas (1889)
Shortly after Grant's 75th birthday, post commander Col. Nelson A. Miles organized a committee to raise a monument at Fort Leavenworth. Soldiers and civilians on post, as well as leading citizens from Kansas and Missouri, raised $5,000 to commission Lorado Taft, who won an international award for his work at the Columbian Exhibition in 1893. Taft created a standing sculpture of Grant atop a similarly sized granite pedestal. The statue was placed near the original front entrance of the fort and dedicated with Senator R. S. Ingalls of Kansas as the speaker.

(way)

Galena, Illinois (1890)
Financed by Chicago *Times-Herald* publisher Herman H. Kohlsaat and sculpted by Danish immigrant Johannes Sopius Gelert, the statue that stands in Grant's hometown of Galena, Illinois, portrays Grant as a private citizen. Grant's widow, Julia Dent Grant, approved of a model for the statue, and the Galena City Council set aside park land for the monument. The statue was dedicated on June 3, 1891, and more recently complimented by a nearby statue of Julia Dent Grant installed at the Grant home in 2006.

Lincoln Park, Chicago (1891)
Twenty-five thousand dollars was raised in private subscription to fund Chicago's eighteen-foot high monument to Grant. Louis T. Rebisso sculpted the equestrian statue and Chicago's Hallowell Granite Company constructed the very large base. The monument sits at the eastern edge of Lincoln Park, overlooking Lake Michigan, and shares the park with other statues and a zoo.

(loc)

Soldiers and Sailors Memorial Arch, Grand Army Plaza, Brooklyn (1893)
William O'Donovan's bronzes of Grant and Lincoln occupy the inner abutments of John Duncan's Soldiers and Sailors Memorial Arch (Duncan was also the architect for Grant's Tomb). President Lincoln turns towards the viewer with his stovepipe hat off in greeting, reaching out to the populace as politicians do. In contrast, Grant looks straight ahead, concentrating on the objective in front of him. Duncan featured Grant with a pensive expression familiar to those who had seen him contemplate issues during the war and his presidency.

(cm)

Columbus, Ohio (1893)
"These are My Jewels" is a Civil War monument in Columbus, Ohio, designed by Levi Scofield. The monument features statues of William Tecumseh Sherman, U.S. Grant, Salmon P. Chase, James A. Garfield, Rutherford B. Hayes, Edwin Stanton and Phillip Sheridan. According to the Cincinnati Museum Center, the monument was first exhibited at the Columbian Exposition in Chicago in 1893 and then installed on the capitol grounds in 1894.

(way)

U.S. Capitol Rotunda, Washington, D.C. (1894)

A marble, standing Grant commissioned by the Grand Army of the Potomac occupies a prominent place in the Capitol Rotunda. Here Grant is portrayed by Franklin Simmons as the victor of Appomattox, with a tree stump to place Grant in the field. Grant holds Lee's sword of surrender at his side, even though Grant had not asked for Lee's sword at Appomattox. The piece was originally shipped in 1894 but initially rejected by the Joint Committee on the Library—apparently it depicted Grant as too plump. Simmons sculpted a second version and the final product was installed in the Capitol Rotunda on May 19, 1900, in a ceremony attended by members of Congress, Grant's widow, Julia, and their daughter and grandchildren.

Grant Square, Bedford-Stuyvesant, Brooklyn (1896)

This monument is one of the first large-scale bronzes cast in the United States. Commissioned by the Union Club of Brooklyn, William Ordway Partridge depicts Grant as a down to earth and weary general with his signature wide-brimmed hat. The sculpture was unveiled on April 27, 1896, the 74th anniversary of Grant's birth.

Fairmount Park, Philadelphia (1897)

Daniel Chester French's equestrian statue in Philadelphia's Fairmount Park portrays Grant as a military commander intently surveying the field in front of him. French sculpted Grant with particular detail to the face to convey the thoughtfulness of the moment and framed it with a broad-brimmed hat and the upturned collar of a cape. He partnered with longtime collaborator, Edward Clark Potter, who sculpted Grant's horse. Together the sculptors sought to create a balance between the accuracy of Grant's appearance and the creation of a compelling work that conveyed messages about Grant's character to the viewer. The 1897 statue was dedicated in a ceremony attended by President William McKinley and unveiled by Miss Rosemary Sartoris, Grant's granddaughter.

(lgsf)

Hackley Park, Muskegon, Michigan (1900)
Local businessman and philanthropist Charles Hackley created a memorial Civil War park, with a soldiers monument in the center. For Memorial Day in 1900, he added statues of Lincoln, Farragut, Sherman, and Grant at the corners. The Grant statue was designed by J. Masset Rhind, who also did work on Grant's Tomb, and cost approximately $6,400.

(way)

Golden Gate Park, San Francisco, California (circa 1904)
A bust of Grant sits in San Francisco's Golden Gate State Park near the DeYoung Museum. The bronze sculpture by Rupert Schmid sits on a granite base originally cut by convicts from Folsom Prison. The stonecutters union balked, and controversy erupted. The base was recut. Controversy also rose over the monument's $8,000 price tag. Because of all the trouble, dedication dates are hard to pin down: 1894, 1896, and 1904.

Capitol Building, Springfield, Illinois (1915)
An eight-foot-high hollow bronze statue of Grant is perched on a corbel in the capitol rotunda below the inner dome. Grant is one of eight figures by artists Peter Poli, Edward Guitink and William Mali that grace the rotunda.

(cm)

Vicksburg National Military Park (1918)

Dedicated in 1919, this $34,000 bronze equestrian statue was commissioned by the state of Illinois and cast by the Florentine Brotherhood Foundry in Chicago. Sculptor Frederick C. Hibbard depicted Grant on his favorite horse "Kangaroo," which he rode extensively during the Vicksburg campaign. "Kangaroo" was a gift from aide Colonel Clark B. Lagow, who acquired the horse after the battle of Shiloh and knew that Grant admired the valuable mount.

(pt)

Long Branch (1918)

Grant declared Long Branch, New Jersey, the nation's "summer capital," and in subsequent years, six other presidents spent considerable time there: Rutherford B. Hayes, Chester A. Arthur, Benjamin Harrison, William McKinley, Woodrow Wilson, and James Garfield (who died there after being shot two-and-a-half months earlier). A monument to the presidents is NOT located at Seven Presidents Oceanfront Park, however, but rather near Pier Village along Long Branch's promenade. A statue of Garfield dominates, but each of the other presidents have markers of their own.

(cm)

National Mall, Washington, D.C. (1922)

Perhaps the biggest tribute to Grant stands in front of the U.S. Capitol on the National Mall where sculptor Henry Merwin Shrady captured Ulysses S. Grant as a Civil War military commander. Sitting atop a 22-foot-high marble pedestal, Grant hunkers down on his horse, Cincinnati. He is not sitting erect in a glorified manner, but is portrayed in the resolute and determined pose of a commander surveying his troops in the midst of battle. The equestrian statue is guarded by reclining lions and flanked by two bronze action sculptures. These two pieces depict groups of cavalry and artillery troops in dramatic action, a more visceral portrayal than other contemporary

statues. The monument is a memorial both to Grant and the men he commanded—a memorial to all those who sacrificed in the war. Shrady was a little-known sculptor when he submitted his design to the monument committee. His design was unlike any of the others submitted, and it is significant that potential rivals Augustus Saint Gaudens and Daniel Chester French were among the judges awarding Shrady the $250,000 commission. Sadly, the 20 years of labor it took to complete the memorial killed the sculptor.

Guinea-Bissau, Africa (circa 1955)

This standing sculpture of Grant as president was commissioned in recognition of Grant's 1870 arbitration of a dispute between Portugal and Great Britain over the former colony. The Portugese government commissioned sculptor Manuel Pereira da Silva to create the monument, which was erected in the main square of Guinea-Bissau's capital city, Bissau. It later survived the wave of destruction that destroyed many of the other monuments representing the nation's colonial past. In August 2007, however, the Grant sculpture disappeared and was discovered in pieces, probably for use as scrap metal. Police were able to recover all of the pieces except Grant's head, but they still hope to recover that piece and reassemble the statue.

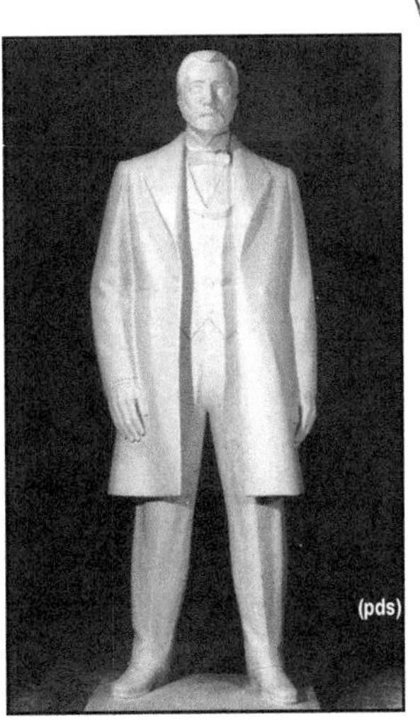

(usgbh)

(usgbh)

Georgetown, Ohio (2004, 2014)
Grant's boyhood home is the only place in America outside Washington, D.C., that has more than one statue of Grant (the bas-relief in Brooklyn counts as a sculpture, not a statue). A bronze statue stands in front of the veteran's home (above, left). Erected in 2004, it was the gift of an anonymous donor. A white granite statue, on a black base stands in the courthouse square (above, right). Called "The Native Son," it was sculpted by Eric Oderg and dedicated in 2012.

(hmdb)

Fort Defiance Park, Cairo, Illinois (circa 2006)
Fort Defiance Park, operated by the city of Cairo, marks the location of a Civil War supply base that sat at the confluence of the Ohio and Mississippi rivers. Grant used the location as his jumping-off point for his expeditions southward. A Grant statue installed there in the late 2000s between the visitor center and the police station was knocked over in 2014; the city put it into storage for safe-keeping.

Rapid City, South Dakota (2008)
The South Dakota city has statues of all of the presidents standing downtown, but Grant's statue remembers him primarily as a military leader. He wears his Union dress uniform and holds a cigar, and he leans against a pedestal that lists his Civil War resume. The statue, sculpted by John Lopez, stands at the corner of 4th St. and Main.

Ulysses S. Grant keeps watch over Brooklyn. (cm)

Appendix co-author KATHLEEN LOGOTHETIS THOMPSON *is a former editor with Emerging Civil War and a Ph.D. student at the University of West Virginia.*

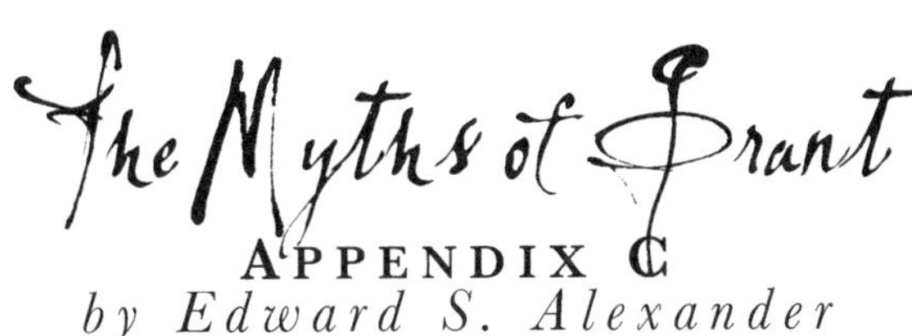

APPENDIX C
by Edward S. Alexander

"Let the North honor the stubborn persistence of Grant;" declared a Petersburg resident after the war, "but the whole world pays greater honor to the unshrinkable nerve of Lee." In the 150 years since the Civil War raged, her bold words have rung true. The legacy of Ulysses S. Grant—the architect of the ultimate victory—has been slandered with accusations of drunken butchery while his marquee antagonist, Robert E. Lee, has been elevated up as a granite god.

In some respects, it all boils down to June 3, 1864. The legacy of Ulysses S. Grant cannot escape that day. After a continuous month of combat starting May 5 in the Wilderness—stretching onward through Spotsylvania Court House to the banks of the North Anna before culmination at the doorstep of Richmond, Virginia—Union high command believed they finally had their counterparts under in the Army of Northern Virginia stretched to their limit.

Brief success in frontal assaults west of the crossroads at Cold Harbor on June 1 convinced Grant that the next day's final push along the same ground could deliver the long awaited prize of the Confederate capital. Delays while maneuvering into position postponed the attack until June 3, precious time for Lee to rally reinforcements to the threatened section. The climactic battle resulted in a lopsided defeat for the Federals and a permanent black mark on Grant's resume. "I have always regretted that the last assault at Cold Harbor was ever made," Grant declared in his memoirs. His later decisions affirmed that statement.

Why is Cold Harbor any more a referendum on Grant's generalship than similar mistakes by the South's premier commander? If we are to summarize Grant's entire military career with the assault at Cold Harbor, shouldn't we do the same for Robert E. Lee and his ill-calculated attack two years previous at nearby Malvern Hill? After vicious assaults forced George B. McClellan's army away from Richmond in late June 1862, Lee believed his adversary had

Serene today, the killing fields of Cold Harbor once generated enough carnage to earn Grant the ignoble nickname "Grant the Butcher." (cm)

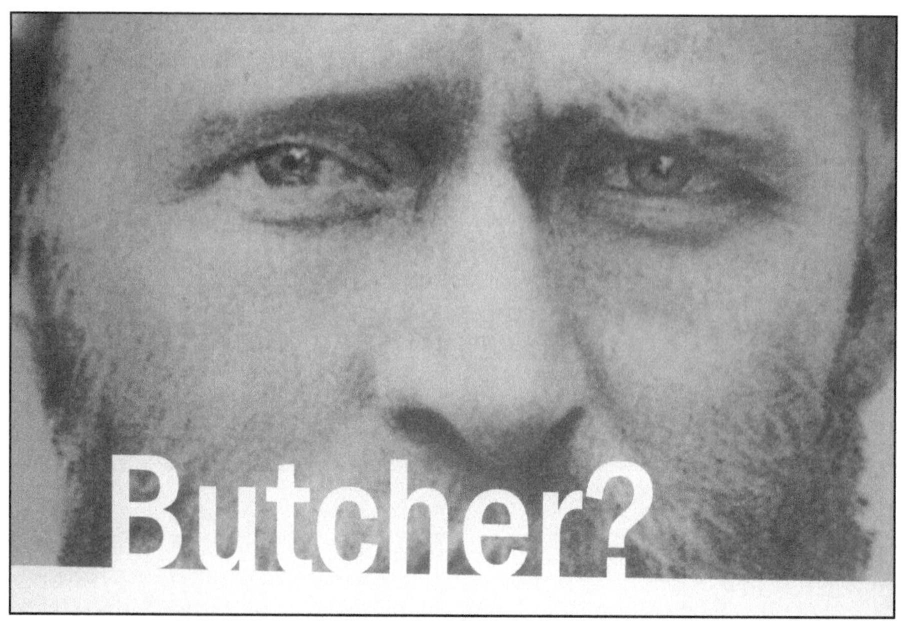

An excellent display at the Ulysses S. Grant Historic Site in St. Louis explores the criticisms most commonly leveled against Grant. One of the most notable such criticisms has been "Grant the Butcher." Grant refused to publicly defend himself against such accusations, the Park Service says, but privately, Grant told a friend: "They call me a butcher, but do you know I sometimes could hardly bring myself to give an order of battle. When I contemplated the death and misery that were sure to follow, I stood appalled." The Park Service goes on to explain that [t]he label stuck with Southern whites' promotion of the Lost Cause ideology: Confederate loss, in part, resulted from the North's (and specifically Grant's) willingness to use its overwhelming manpower, regardless of the cost in human lives." (bp)

reached a breaking point. Despite the failure of the preliminary artillery barrage to soften the Union defenses, 35,000 Confederate soldiers slowly ascended the gentle slopes in piecemeal fashion; 5,650 of that number fell dead or wounded on the field, compared to just over 2,000 for the Union.

"It was not war, it was murder," recalled division commander D. H. Hill of Malvern Hill in a succinct assessment that is more frequently used to describe Grant's tactics. "As for Malvern Hill, who is going to tell the truth about it," wrote Hill's colleague Lafayette McLaws. He believed that Southerners would denounce him as a traitor if he ever gave his full recollections of the battle.

One could argue that being backed up against his capital left Lee no choice but to adopt bold, aggressive tactics to force the Union away. But later battles where circumstances did not require such audacious assaults stand witness to Lee's obstinate refusal to realize the Union army could stand up to his withering blows. After suffering more than 13,000 casualties at Chancellorsville, the strategic picture essentially remained the same for the Confederates. Two months later, Lee lost between 23,000-28,000 men in his failed Northern invasion that culminated with nearly 7,000 casualties in Pickett's doomed charge on Cemetery Ridge.

Compare Lee's unflinching audacity with the infamous assault at Cold Harbor and the impact it had on Ulysses S. Grant. Certainly the Union soldiers who actually participated in the charge that morning suffered tremendously, but their losses are far lower than is commonly cited. "Nobody knows the exact figures of casualties in the first wave," claimed author Clifford Dowdey around the war's centennial, yet he still offered a guess: "Within less than an hour more than seven thousand men fell, killed or wounded, in moving against a fire power so uniform in its destructiveness that no living thing could advance in the face of it."

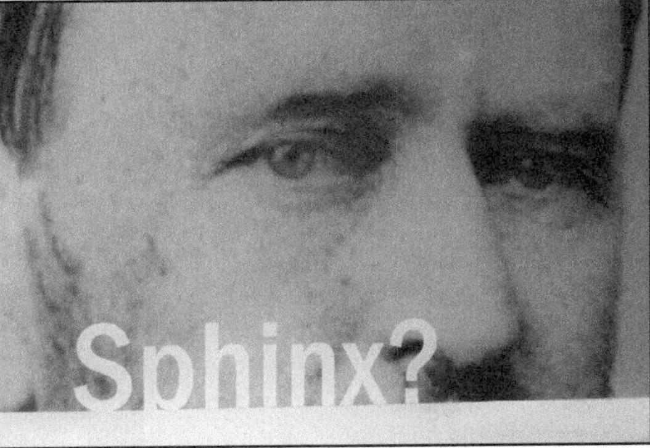

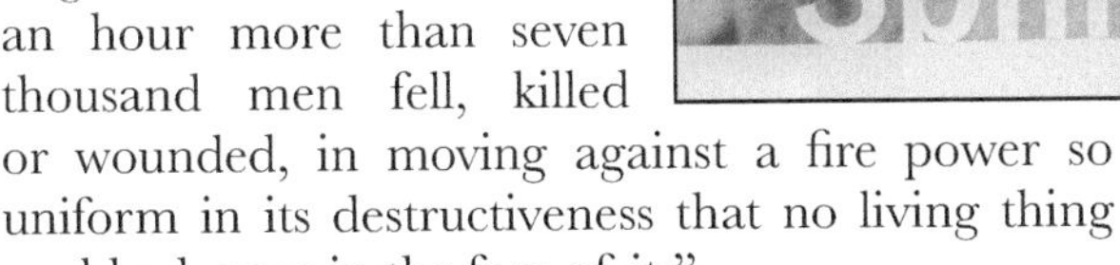

"During the Civil War," The National Park Service explains, "Grant was called 'Grant the Sphinx' and 'Ulysses the Silent.' The sobriquets, when applied in a negative manner, equated his silence with stupidity. Quiet by nature, Grant's distaste for public speaking developed early in his military career. He seldom publicly defended himself or let others talk on his behalf. Believing rebuttals only added credence to accusations, he chose to let his actions speak for him. As a result, Grant remains something of an enigma, confounding historians who try to interpret the meaning of his silence." (bp)

Dowdey's estimate fell in line with traditional analysis and scrutiny about Grant's blunder. But recent scholarship by Gordon C. Rhea suggests that the Union suffered only 3,500 in killed and wounded during the grand assault, or half those suffered during Pickett's Charge. The commonly quoted 7,000 number is the result of postwar writers summarizing the entire day's fighting, which included constant artillery and sharpshooter fire across the lengthy front, later Confederate counterattacks, and fighting on other sections of the line. The defeat nevertheless cost Grant dearly at the time.

Aside from these new accusations of "Grant the Butcher," the Union commander already battled against the label of "Grant the Drunk." These rumors contained an element of truth. Grant admitted his own biggest weakness with alcohol: "Sometimes I can drink freely without any unpleasant effect; at others I cannot take even a single glass of light wine."

Before the war he clearly struggled with alcohol during the lonely, boring stints with the Regular Army that separated him from his wife Julia. He also occasionally tried to self-medicate other ailments, like recurring migraine headaches, with liquor. However Grant's battles with the bottle are hardly a unique story among the soldiers on the frontier. When he had the loving support of his family, a clean bill of health, and a clear mission to focus on, alcohol was not a problem. "If Grant was an alcoholic," claims historian James McPherson, "he should have felt pride . . . because he overcame his illness to achieve success and fame without the support system of modern medicine and organizations like Alcoholics Anonymous."

Charges of prejudice against Grant stem mostly from his infamous Order No. 11, issued December 17, 1862. It immediately raised a storm of controversy, and Grant revoked the order on January 6. "Used afterwards to demonstrate his bigotry in general, the order illustrates neither a deep prejudice nor freedom from the stereotypes of this day," says the NPS. (bp)

During the Civil War, when brief spells of inactivity or illness left the general vulnerable to temptation, Grant's chief of staff John Rawlins stepped up to keep the general sober. Rumors nevertheless shadowed his meteoric rise in the Western Theater. These accusations, however, were largely fueled by his jealous military rivals, and it is clear that alcohol did not have a direct impact upon his generalship.

But public prominence brings its fair share of scrutiny, and the "Savior of the Union" was frequently dogged with critical labels. His hard times in civilian life before the war led critics to consider him "Grant the Failure." His infamous Order No. 11 in December 1862, expelling Jews from his military district, earned him ire as "Grant the Racist." The corruption surrounding his presidency garnered him criticism as "Grant the Incompetent."

"Perceptions of Grant as an incompetent president can be directly attributed to the scandals exposed during his presidency, involving members of his cabinet, public officials, and individuals with whom Grant was acquainted," the NPS explains. (bp)

His detractors' most common critique, then and to this day, remains that of "Grant the Butcher." However, this is based off an oversimplification of the final year of the war. Grant's Overland Campaign did reap a terrible death, but when victory seemed to fall out of grasp while knocking on Richmond's door in June 1864, the general forged a new path to victory by adapting his tactics.

Recognizing that the Cold Harbor line could

not be broken, Grant turned his gaze 20 miles south of Richmond to the crucial railroad junction of Petersburg. He hoped a swift move on Petersburg would deprive the Confederate army and capital of food, supplies, and communications with their dwindling nation. The campaign to capture the Cockade City devolved into a nine-and-a-half-month ordeal, the sheer length of which stymies historians. "The story of Petersburg will never be written," claimed a North Carolina soldier who experienced the entire campaign, "volumes would be required to contain it, and even those who went through the trying ordeal, can not recall a satisfactorily outline of the weird and graphic occurrences of that stormy period."

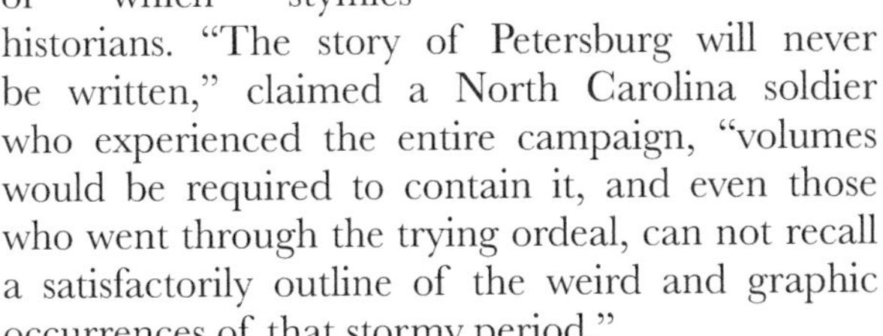

Grant's critics like to portray him as a drunk—a charge that had dogged him for decades. While credible reports do exist of Grant having too much to drink on a few occasions, they were blown out of proportion by political rivals in and out of the military; they used the age-old accusation of "drunk" to discredit Grant while bolstering their own agendas. (bp)

Due to the challenging nature to grasp and recognize the subtle nuances mastered by Grant in the campaign, his performance for the full duration of the campaign is still often summarized in line with the myth that emerged at Cold Harbor—that he simply aimed to hammer away at Lee with his overwhelming numbers until there were no Confederates left to shoot down his mass attackers. In reality, Grant authorized just a few frontal assaults: in the middle of June, hoping to seize the city before Lee's army could be transferred down from Richmond; the infamous debacle after the explosion at the Crater in late July; and the final assault in early April 1865 that did succeed is wresting control of Petersburg from the Confederacy.

In the meantime, he used deft maneuvering across a front extending from east of Richmond to southwest of Petersburg to confuse Lee as to where the next offensive would occur while harnessing the logistical advantages of the Northern military industrial complex in a modern way of warfare that the South simply could not keep pace with.

Are we to punish Grant for recognizing and utilizing the advantages he had?

EDWARD ALEXANDER ***is a park ranger at Pamplin Historical Park in Petersburg, Virginia. Author of the ECWS book*** **Dawn of Victory: Breakthrough at Petersburg,** ***Edward is also a contributor for Emerging Civil War***

The Grant Administration

APPENDIX D

by Richard G. Frederick

Everyone knows the old joke question about who's buried in Grant's Tomb. After reviewing a cross-section of the literature on the Grant administration, however, the reader can only conclude that the famous question is actually more of a conundrum than a simplistic riddle. Who indeed is that guy in the tomb? Is he the worst president who ever lived? Or is he some vastly underrated figure who has tragically been exiled to presidential irrelevancy with the likes of Harding and Pierce? If the latter is the case, how did this gross miscarriage of historiography occur? Was it the venal jealousy of his contemporaries? The flawed perceptions of more recent writers? A course of catastrophic events over which he had no control?

Grant's presidency seemed to begin auspiciously enough, with a landslide election. Grant and his running mate, Schuyler Colfax, received 214 of the 294 electoral college ballots, handily defeating the Democrats Horatio Seymour and Francis P. Blair. Upon closer examination, the election was much narrower, with a popular majority of only 300,000 for the Republican ticket; the newly enfranchised African-American vote made the difference, with more than 700,000 blacks casting votes.

In retrospect, it is easy to picture Grant as the old grizzled war veteran, the senior statesman among ranking generals with his four stars. It is just as easy to forget that Grant was still only 46, the youngest elected president in his day. He set out on a dynamic course, one that featured, he hoped, his independence from the politicos and their internecine power struggles.

He first determined to set his own mark on the cabinet. Without consulting the Republican leadership, and largely to their chagrin, he selected the men he thought would serve him, using as a model the subsidiary staff positions in the military. Nearly all presidents, on their own or in collusion with leaders of their parties, have chosen cabinets with some excellent personnel and some mediocre appointments. Grant's was no exception.

Grant still stands vigil in Washington, D.C. in front of the Capitol. (cm)

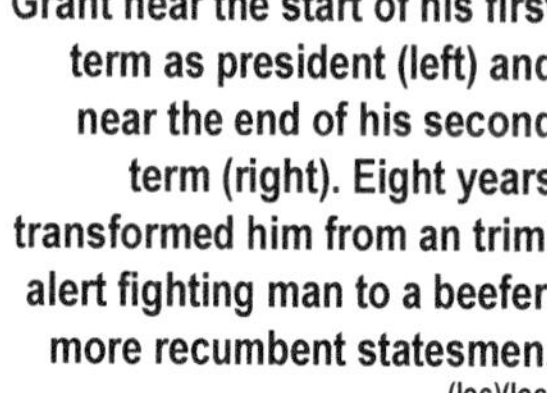

Grant near the start of his first term as president (left) and near the end of his second term (right). Eight years transformed him from an trim, alert fighting man to a beefer, more recumbent statesmen. (loc)(loc)

One mistake was his appointment as Secretary of Treasury of Alexander T. Stewart, a New York department store owner who pioneered many of the sales and marketing techniques associated with giants like Macy's somewhat later. It turned out that Stewart, as "a merchant," was invalidated from holding the post by an 80-year-old Congressional statute. When the president asked Congress for an exception, the leaders he had rebuffed with his independent appointments refused. In Grant's favor, his new appointee for the post, George Boutwell, was both able and, as a long-standing member of the House of Representatives, acceptable to Congressional Republicans.

Grant addressed what he saw as the major issues faced by his administration in his first inaugural address. The four areas he specifically noted were economic stabilization, Indian reform, the continued reconstruction of the South, especially including the passage of a voting rights amendment for blacks, and securing a stronger place for the United States in world affairs.

Grant's vision of a stronger economy focused on ridding the country of debt, especially through the retirement of the paper money, or "greenbacks," issued as an emergency funding measure during the Civil War. In line with the fiscal conservative thinking of the day, Grant was a "sound money" man who equated a strong economy with strict adherence to the gold standard. This was the basis of the Public Credit Act of 1869, which decreed that all public debts would be paid in gold. This opened the door for the infamous attempt by a pair

Railroad men Jay Gould (left) and Jim Fisk (right) tried to corner the gold market; Grant foiled them. Imagine the extra symbolism, then, of the golden spike Grant drove in the ground to complete the Trans-Continental Railroad. Years later, when Buck Grant began suspecting Ferdinand Ward's duplicity, he took Grant & Ward's books to Gould for review. Gould immediately realized the firm's holdings were worthless. (loc)(loc)

of Wall Street scoundrels, Jim Fisk and Jay Gould, to corner the gold market. Their use of Grant's rather dim-witted brother-in-law in the scheme convinced some that the president was involved in the shady manipulations, even though he stopped the attempt by ordering the Treasury to flood the market with gold, and was later absolved of any wrong-doing by a Congressional investigation.

Grant's continued deflationary policies after 1869 hurt farmers and other debtors, leading to a "Greenback" political movement and a short-lived third party. In addition, these policies contributed to the severity of the depression of the 1870s, which began as a result of instability in railroad securities and defaults by several railroads. After backing a reissue of $26 million in greenbacks to stimulate the economy, Grant retreated to a sound money policy in 1874 and backed the Resumption Act of 1875, which redeemed greenbacks in gold at face value. Ruthless deflation during a time of expanding production and population proved to be both unpopular and largely unsuccessful.

Indian policy during the Grant years was largely dictated by the economic development of the West. Railroads, minerals, and farming were the keys. The completion of the first transcontinental railroad in 1869 led to a flurry of activity among railroad magnates to establish a rail network through the trans-Mississippi region. Similarly, gold and silver strikes from California eastward into adjacent territories brought in large populations of white settlers, followed closely by homesteaders. All of these incursions impacted the Plains Indians, who found themselves constantly crowded into fewer areas.

Grant's approach to the "Indian problem" was widely considered the most humanitarian approach of the day, but it proved to be one that led to bitterness and continued warfare. The key was the "civilization" of the Indians—their conversion to the white way of life. This meant concentration on reservations and education in the white man's ways, especially for the children, who would grow up to become farmers and live in nuclear families. Until they became truly self-sufficient in their new lifestyle, the government would take care of them by providing all manner of supplies, including food, to the reservations.

When Robert E. Lee saw Ely Parker in the McClean parlor with Grant at Appomattox, he shook the Seneca's hand and said, "I am glad to see one real American here." Parker replied, "We are all Americans." (nps)

Unfortunately, corruption became the rule of the day, with Indian agents routinely robbing the government and their Indian charges by selling products meant for the Indians or by providing them with vastly inferior products than those the government paid for. Grant's appointment of his former military aide, Gen. Ely S. Parker, a member of the Seneca tribe, as Commissioner of Indian Affairs had little effect on stemming the corruption. The parlous state of affairs on the reservations, along with the trespassing of gold miners on treaty-guaranteed Indian lands in the Black Hills, led to military confrontations during the Grant administration, notably Little Big Horn in 1876.

Grant proved to be a staunch supporter of the Radical Republicans during the ongoing process of Reconstruction. He especially pointed to the necessity of black suffrage, which was guaranteed by the Fifteenth Amendment, passed by the states in 1870. The ratification was also marked by the rise of white terrorist groups such as the Ku Klux Klan, however. Grant acted decisively against such groups, backing the Enforcement Acts of 1870 and 1871, which allowed for the use of Federal troops and martial law not only in unreconstructed regions but also in states that had been reconstructed and returned to the Union. After the passage of the Ku Klux Klan Act, Federal troops helped root out the organization in North Carolina. In South Carolina, at the urging of Attorney General Amos T. Ackerman, Grant proclaimed a "condition of lawlessness" in several counties that served as a Klan stronghold. The writ

Grant signed a bill intended to suppress the growing power of the KKK. (loc)

of habeas corpus was suspended and hundreds of arrests were made, which effectively broke the back of the Klan in the region.

The Republican party became polarized over the issue of Reconstruction during the 1870s, with the majority coming to favor its end. Grant's actions mirrored this divide. He ordered Gen. Philip Sheridan to put down an insurrection against the Reconstruction government of Louisiana in 1874, but refused to take action in a similar event in Mississippi the following year. Like others in the Republican hierarchy, he was willing to accept the Thirteenth, Fourteenth, and Fifteenth Amendments as adequate protection for the rights of freed slaves in the South, in spite of indications to the contrary.

The major foreign affairs matter—a treaty with Great Britain—was a triumph for the administration. The major reason for opening negotiations on the American side was the case against Great Britain for claims against British-built commerce raiders sold to the Confederacy during the Civil War. An earlier treaty had been rejected by the Senate, led by the strident Charles Sumner, who demanded unrealistic collateral damage claims in the billions of dollars. There were other important considerations between the countries as well, including navigation rights on rivers and the Great Lakes between the United States and Canada and an exact drawing of the boundary between the two countries on the west coast.

Secretary of State Hamilton Fish expertly guided the negotiations. The result was the Treaty of Washington, which was quickly approved by the U.S. Senate in May of 1871. Boundaries were determined once and for all, agreement was reached on United States fishing privileges in Canada, and three principles were established (and became part of international law) regarding damage claims resulting from commerce raiding. The amount of damages was not determined by the negotiators in Washington, but was set for arbitration by an international panel the following year in Geneva. The final tally set there was $15,500,000, an enormous amount at the time. Thanks largely to this achievement, which opened a new era of friendship between the United States and Great Britain, Fish is generally regarded as one of the most outstanding Secretaries of State.

Grant remained loyal to aide Orville Babcock through the Whiskey Ring scandal—an example of Grant's loyalty blinding him to reality. "Although historians have repeatedly asserted Grant's innocence," says the NPS, "they have also blamed him for being politically naive in continuing to associate with those under investigation." (loc)

Looked at from the standpoint of major issues and policies, the Grant administration is a mixed bag. But these issues are not the ones that grab attention in the textbooks and general accounts of the Gilded Age. The Grant legacy—sometimes referred to as "Grantism"—is often seen as one of corruption, scandals, loose morals, and flagrant materialism. Mention of the Grant presidency elicits comparisons with Harding and discussions of Credit Mobilier, Fisk and Gould's gold manipulations, frauds in the Indian Bureau, and the Whisky Ring. It was a particularly corrupt era in politics and other areas in America, and the Grant administration was squarely in the middle of numerous exposes.

Richard Frederick, Ph.D., ***is the author of books on Warren G. Harding and William Howard Taft ("So I know about outstanding presidents," he deadpans). He has taught U.S. history at the University of Pittsburgh at Bradford since 1979, and is a past recipient of the university-wide Chancellor's Distinguished Teaching Award.***

Of course, there was a great deal of hyperbole in contemporary newspaper accounts, many of which were politically motivated. One could argue that Grant himself was never implicated in any wrongdoing. If he was guilty of anything, it was his steadfastness in standing by his friends. The Whisky Ring case was a good example. In St. Louis and other areas, tax collectors conspired with distillers

to defraud the government of tax revenue. When a local newspaper exposed the arrangement, Congress investigated, and more than 200 people were indicted, including Grant's personal secretary, Gen. O. E. Babcock. Grant rushed to Babcock's defense, for a while insisting that he testify at his friend's trial in St. Louis. While his friends prevailed upon him to stay in Washington, he defended Babcock during a five-hour deposition before Babcock's attorneys, the attorney general, and Chief Justice Morrison R. Waite. With Grant's endorsement and a lack of real evidence, Babcock was acquitted.

A far different outcome occurred in the case of William Belknap, Grant's secretary of war, who was accused of receiving bribes in connection with the operation of trading posts on Indian land. Although he quickly resigned his post early in 1876 to avoid impeachment, there was little doubt as to his guilt. Opposition newspapers hurried to remind voters in the presidential election year that this was but one in a series of Grant appointees that were disgraced by public exposures.

Ulysses S. Grant was an early example of the "outsider" who became president—one who did not achieve the highest elected position in the country by coming through the legislature or serving as governor of a state. While this allowed him to make decisions independently, it also brought with it a certain naiveté about how to get things done. This was especially crucial in the politically charged era of Reconstruction.

As to the scandals so freely associated with Grant, people who served with him, as well as later biographers, have always emphasized his personal integrity, insisting that men he trusted took advantage of their positions to advance their personal gain. While this may be true, the fact is that history has not looked kindly on presidents unable to discriminate in choosing subordinates with character. Harding's venal friends and Nixon's thugs have brought general disregard to positive achievements in those presidencies, as have Credit Mobilier and the Whisky Ring to Grant's.

LOOKING ONLY AT THE SCANDALS OF GRANT'S ADMINISTRATIONS PROVIDES AN INCOMPLETE LOOK, SAYS THE NATIONAL PARK SERVICE. "GRANT'S OWN EVALUATION," THE NPS POINTS OUT, "INCLUDED EXAMINING HIS ABILITY TO IMPLEMENT HIS DOMESTIC AND FOREIGN POLICIES, TAKING PRIDE IN ACCOMPLISHMENTS WHILE ACKNOWLEDGING SOME FAILURES."

TWAIN
APR. 21 1910

The Unlikely Friendship of Grant and Twain

APPENDIX E

by Jim McWilliams

It's perhaps inevitable that two giants of late 19th century America, Mark Twain and Ulysses S. Grant, should meet and become friends after they both became famous, but who would have guessed that their paths had nearly crossed some two decades earlier, when they fought on opposite sides in the Civil War? Sometimes fact is stranger than fiction.

Mark Twain, born Samuel L. Clemens on November 30, 1835, in northeast Missouri, grew up never questioning the morality of slavery. In fact, as he recalled in his later years, his church had preached that God "approved" of slavery, a view that he gave to Huckleberry Finn, who is similarly untroubled by the institution until he spends a month on a raft with a kind-hearted slave, Jim. So it is no surprise that when war broke out on April 12, 1861, the now-unemployed riverboat pilot joined the area's Confederate forces, the Marion Rangers, a unit of irregulars. Twain, however, seemed to enlist more as a lark than for any political or ideological reasons, and after a couple of weeks of little food but many mosquitoes, he decided to desert and head west. Helping him make this decision was the rumor (later confirmed) that a Union colonel was leading a regiment into the area with orders to destroy all Confederate guerilla forces. Years later, long after the war, Twain learned that colonel's name: Ulysses S. Grant.

Twain and Grant had their first physical meeting at a reception in Washington D.C. in 1866, but they apparently did little more than shake hands. They then met briefly at the White House during Grant's first term as president (again for just a minute although Twain managed to tell Grant that he felt "embarrassed") before finally meeting more substantially on November 13, 1879, when Twain was scheduled to deliver a speech at a Chicago banquet honoring the Army of the Tennessee and its former commander. In his speech, not delivered

Mark Twain is buried in Woodlawn Cemetery in Elmira, New York—his wife's hometown. A monument stands at the head of the family plot, and visitors frequently leave cigars on Twain's headstone. (cm)

until after 2 a.m. the next day, Twain joked that even the great Grant, like every other man in the hall, was once nothing more than a squalling baby trying to get his big toe into his mouth. After a long pause, he then produced this punch line: "And if the child is but a prophecy of the man, there are mighty few who will doubt that he succeeded." No one laughed louder or longer than Grant.

Biographer Justin Kaplan referred to Twain as "a Grant-intoxicated man." (loc)

The two men then became friends and enjoyed many long conversations, especially in Grant's home in New York City, and when the ex-president was feeling particularly depressed by his bleak financial situation in 1881, he confided to Twain that he might need to sell his personal possessions to pay his debts. Twain, horrified that such a great man could be in this plight, encouraged him to write his memoirs, arguing that they would not just restore his finances but also redeem his good name following the political scandals that had plagued his second presidential term. Grant, however, insisted that he wasn't a writer and refused Twain's entreaties. He continued to resist turning to the pen until he had exhausted all other avenues of raising money and had also been diagnosed with terminal throat cancer.

When he agreed to write an article about the battle at Shiloh for the Century, Grant discovered he enjoyed writing it, so he began negotiations for his memoirs. He worried that entering business with Twain might affect their friendship), but, finally, in February 1885, Grant agreed to sign with him. He felt gratified when his friend then had attorneys draft the contract in such a way that creditors couldn't seize any royalties even after his death.

Grant, knowing that his cancer would soon kill him and that his financial situation was growing ever more precarious, then worked virtually non-stop on his memoirs. His wife, Julia; his son, Frederick; and his friend (and former staff officer) Adam Badeau assisted him with editing and proofreading. Twain, too, rendered great help, both in literary advice and in encouragement to keep working through the illness. Twain also worked behind the scenes at the publishing company to ensure that the memoirs would be properly marketed and advertised; he even personally approved the quality of paper for the pages.

Jim McWilliams, Ph.D., ***professor of English and chair of the Department of Language and Literature at Dickinson State University, is the author or editor of four books, including two about Mark Twain.***

With Grant's battle with cancer coming to its inevitable conclusion, Twain rushed to the printers the first volume of the memoirs just as soon as the copyediting was complete. That first volume, covering Grant's childhood through the Vicksburg campaign, came out on December 1, 1885, and received almost universally enthusiastic reviews, but Grant himself did not live to see its publication, for he had died on July 23. (Twain had last visited him, at a summer cottage in Saratoga Springs, New York, on July 2.) The second volume came out on May 10, 1886, and was equally well received. Grant's estate received approximately $450,000 in royalties, while Twain's profits were approximately $200,000.

During the same period Grant worked on his memoirs, Twain did much of his writing in a specially constructed "octagonal study" at his wife's family's farm in Elmira, New York (top). In 1952, the study was relocated to the campus of Elmira College, where it remains open to visitors during the summer and by appointment during the off-season (above). (loc)(cm)

One controversy through the years, beginning even before the volumes were actually published, is that a number of critics have alleged, without much concrete evidence, that Grant didn't write his own memoirs. Most of these allegations have targeted Badeau, who wrote an 1881 book about Grant's military campaigns, or Twain as being the true author. Although both men certainly helped edit and proofread Grant's manuscript, the scholarly consensus is that Grant did indeed write his own memoirs. It's worth noting that Grant severed his relationship with Badeau in a dispute about his compensation for his editorial help.

Twain felt proud to have been associated, personally and professionally, with Grant, a man he called "the greatest" he had ever met. In response to the occasionally heated debate in about where Grant should be buried (later resolved in favor of New York City), Twain simply said in a July 30, 1885, letter to the New York Sun, "Wherever Grant's body lies, that is national ground."

Suggested Reading

Grant's Last Battle

The Last Days of General Grant
Adam Badeau
Wetware Media, LLC (2010)
ASIN: B0043M4NUO

The final chapter of Badeau's *Grant in Peace* (1887), "The Last Days of General Grant" is written in the florid purple prose of an affected, self-styled litterateur. Melodramatic style aside, though, Badeau was one of Grant's intimates and had a front-row seat to Grant's decline—and Grant's understated literary genius.

Grant's Final Victory: Ulysses S. Grant's Heroic Last Year
Charles Bracelen Flood
DaCapo (2012)
ISBN-13: 978-0306821516

Flood is one of the best modern Civil War storytellers, able to sustain a novel-length, novel-like account of Grant's final chapter. Interspersed are key moments from Grant's military and political history, creating a multi-layered tapestry built on excellent research and effective structure. There is much to like about this book.

Many Are the Hearts: The Agony and Triumph of Ulysses S. Grant.
Richard Goldhurst
Reader's Digest Press (1973)
ISBN: 0-88349-050-1

"The facts of Grant's life and career are so indisputable as to need no documentation," Goldhurst writes in an introductory author's note, which sets the tone for a Shelby Foote-esque narrative. Perry and Flood both draw heavily upon Goldhurst's un-footnoted book, making it the seminal modern account of Grant's last days.

Personal Memoirs of U.S. Grant / Selected Letters
Grant, Ulysses S.
Library of America (1990)
ISBN-13: 978-0940450585

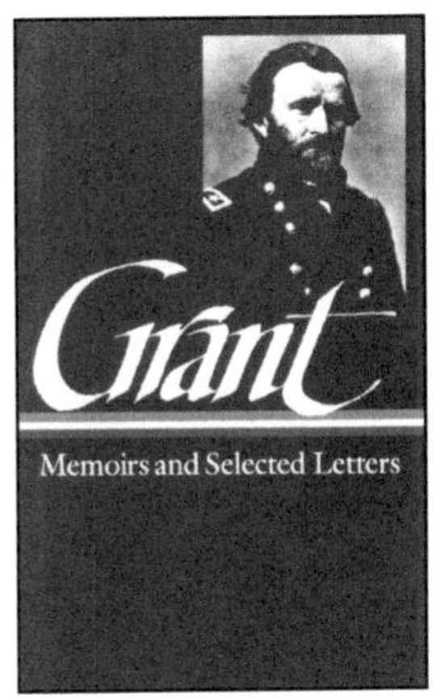

Grant's *Memoirs* have never gone out of print, so there are many easy-to-find editions, and because the book is in the public domain, it's readily available for free. Like all Library of America volumes, though, this one is well worth the money because of its solid binding and handsome design. Pulitzer-winning Grant biographer William McFeely edited the collection, which includes many of Grant's notes to his doctors from his last days, plus an interesting assortment of personal letters.

A Few Stout Individuals
John Guare
Grove Press (2003)
ISBN-13: 978-0739434512
Dramatist Play Service (2003)
ISBN-13: 978-0822219071

The author of *Six Degrees of Separation*, Guare wrote this play about Grant's struggle to write his memoirs after a cad at a dinner party accused him of being uneducated because Guare had never read the memoirs. As a playwright, Guare is able to explore Grant's story in a way traditional historians can't.

Grant & Twain: The Story of an American Friendship
Mark Perry
Random House (2005)
ISBN-13: 978-0812966138

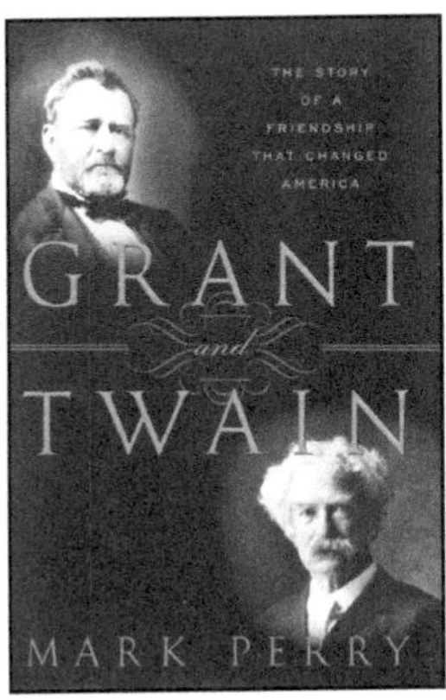

"[A]s Grant was struggling to write the story of his life, he was helped in his final battle by a man who had just completed the story of his," Perry says, referring to the *Memoirs* and *Huck Finn*. "Those two books, perhaps the finest work of American nonfiction ever written and the greatest of all American novels, defined their legacy." Perry is keenly aware that he's telling the tale of two of the most powerful literary figures in American history, and his writing lives up to the exciting challenge.

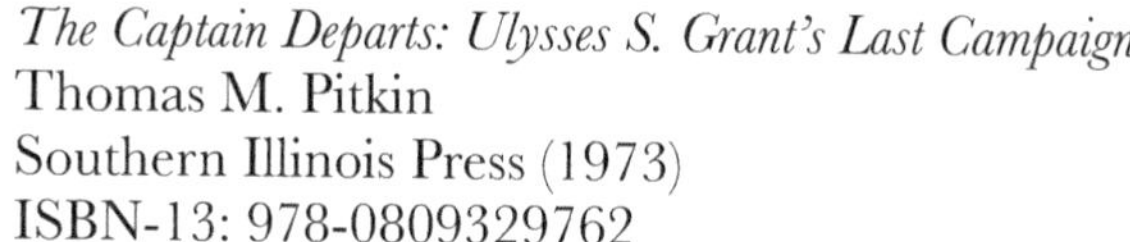

The Captain Departs: Ulysses S. Grant's Last Campaign
Thomas M. Pitkin
Southern Illinois Press (1973)
ISBN-13: 978-0809329762

Pitkin's book began as an "outgrowth of a report on Grant Cottage . . . prepared for the Office of State History, New York State Education Department," and as such, it often reads with all the drama of a government report. It's a clear, condensed account of events, though—a good "next step" from *Grant's Last Battle.*

President Grant Reconsidered
Scaturro, Frank J.
Madison Books (1999)
ISBN-13: 978-1568331324

The most intriguing chapter of Grant's life left unexamined in his memoirs was his presidency. Without his side of the story, history has typically dismissed Grant as a mediocre president surrounded by scandal. Scaturro cautions against the "conventional wisdom" and offers a bold reassessment of Grant's political career.

Saving Grant Cottage: How a Survivor of Andersonville, A Housewife, a Medical Missionary, An Immigrant from Japan (and Others) Saved a Precious Piece of Our History
Steve Trimm
Friends of Grant Cottage (2012)
[no ISBN]

As a living historian, Trimm ably portrays Grant at events at Grant Cottage, where he also guides tours of the building. He lives the story and occupies the space of Grant's last days, so he knows it with an intimacy few people have. Filled with fabulous anecdotes, his wonderful history of the cottage serves as a love letter to those who, like him, have preserved the story and the site.

General Grant and the Rewriting of History: How the Destruction of General William S. Rosecrans Influenced Our Understanding of the Civil War
Frank P. Varney
Savas Beatie (2013)
ISBN-13: 978-1611211184

Varney's fascinating, thoroughly researched look at Grant's memoirs peels back the onion layers to critically examine what Grant does and doesn't say in his account of the war. Grant's book is often accepted as objective history, but Varney points out Grant's political and personal agendas that shape the book as subjective memoir.

U.S. Grant: American Hero, American Myth
Joan Waugh
UNC Press (2009)
ISBN-13: 978-0-8078-3317-9

Grant's feats "attained mythic status and, like many national myths, contained elements of truth and exaggeration, accuracy and distortion," writes Waugh, whose book "traces the shifting legacy of general and president Ulysses S. Grant, who emerged from obscurity to claim victory as the North's greatest military leader." She pays particular attention to Grant's efforts as a memoirist to shape his own legacy and the very meaning of the Civil War.

A Disposition to be Rich: Ferdinand Ward, the Greatest Swindler of the Gilded Age
Geoffrey Ward
Vintage (2013)
ISBN-13: 978-0345804693

Ferdinand Ward appears in Grant's story long enough to ruin him and then typically vanishes, but his descendent, historian Geoffrey Ward (best known for his collaborations with filmmaker Ken Burns), takes time to explore Ward's story in its own right. The book's original subtitle sums it up well: "How a Small-Town Pastor's Son Ruined an American President, Brought on a Wall Street Crash, and Made Himself the Best-Hated Man in the United States."

About the Author

Chris Mackowski, Ph.D., is co-founder and editor-in-chief of Emerging Civil War (www.emergingcivilwar.com); historian-in-residence at Stevenson Ridge, a historic property on the Spotsylvania battlefield (www.stevensonridge.com); and professor of journalism and mass communication at St. Bonaventure University in western New York. He has authored or co-authored twelve books on the Civil War.